Frederick Guttman R.

ESCHATOLOGY OF THE PROPHET DANIEL

First edition. September 19, 2024.

Copyright © 2024 Frederick Guttmann.

ISBN: 979-8231019120

Written by Frederick Guttmann.

ESCHATOLOGY OF THE PROPHET DANIEL

Project Magen

Frederick Guttman R.

www.frederickguttmann.com[1]
Cover: Aday Quintero P.
133 pages
Year 2011 (last update 2015)

---

1. http://www.frederickguttmann.com

Introduction

The prophet Daniel is a historical icon of the people of Israel, although it is more special for Christian theology. It is especially important for being the prophet with the most revelations received in a historical context and even in great detail, addressing global geopolitical issues and conquest centuries before such occurred. Although this man is for Christianity much more than for the Jews themselves, and that is why I have dedicated this work to him, since, unlike what would happen to a greater extent with Judaism, within Christianity he is largely a turning point in eschatology.

The name 'Daniel' means in Hebrew "God is my judge" or "God's judgment", although during his stay in Babel (Babylon) he was called in Akkadian 'Balatsu-usur' ("Bel protects the king"), transliterated into Spanish as 'Beltsasar'. He was one of the sons of the Jewish aristocracy who were taken out of Israel by Nebuchadnezzar II of Babylon, during the time of Iahoikin (Joaquin), king of Judah, that is, he was taken captive around 598 or 597 BC. C., although it is not officially known how old he was when he was taken, or his year of birth itself. Something that recently became known is that the book of Daniel enjoyed great popularity among the essential community, there being a lot of information that emphasizes its writing in the Qumran Caves, even considering it as "canonical" (the Jews did not make it available). Daniel with the compendium of manuscripts of the Nebiim (Prophets) but with the merely historical ones, the Ketubim (Writings)). In fact, if the popularity of a book is judged by the number of copies found in the caves, Daniel - with his 8 scrolls - would occupy the 4th place, together with the book of the 12 prophets (Deuteronomy has 14 manuscripts, Isaías has 12, and the Samos 10).

Despite the criticisms from the Talmud, regarding the true nature of Daniel as a prophet and the accusations against him for giving " *good advice to the king of Babylon* " (which according to Chazal caused him to end up in the den of lions) , his The writings speak for themselves, as does the biblical testimony. As we will see later in chapter 9, especially at the end of it, it would seem that it was in the interest of orthodox Jews to disparage Daniel's work in order to refute the interpretation of his revelation received about the manifestation of the Messiah. Although, Daniel recounts very strong episodes of heavenly intervention and is even cited as one of the "three saints", or most pleasing men in the eyes of God in ancient times:

« *If these three men were in the midst of her, [...] and Noah, Daniel and Job were in the midst of her, as I live, says Yaheveh Adonai, that they would not deliver son or daughter. Only they, for their justice, would spare their own lives.* » (Ezekiel 14:18-20, RVA 95) .

Daniel was part of the noble Jews who were taken to the court of King Nabukanetzar II (name usually transcribed as 'Nebuchadnezzar'). It was at that time that he became famous for revealing to said sovereign the content and interpretation of a dream, and from then on several historical visions followed him until his unknown end (it is not officially known how Daniel's life ended). The historical visions of this Jewish prophet cover the most significant events of his time, and anticipate all the most important things that took place between the great powers that last until the rise of the Roman empire. The context of most of his visions refers to geopolitical and military issues regarding Babylon, then Persia, the Hellenic peoples that would follow after this, and finally the Latins. These issues are verified in at least 5 complete contextual visions highlighting what would become of Nebuchadnezzar, his descendants, the Medo-Persian invasion, the Persian uprising against the West, the Macedonian revenge and attempted Achaemenid response, the Maccabean wars, the Greek submission to Egypt, and the end of the Jews in Judea with the rise of the Roman Empire.

Despite this, it is notorious that there are a couple of verses in the book of Daniel (ex. 7:25-27) that speak of much later coasts, such as the manifestation and work of Belial (the Antichrist) - part of a fourth beast. - as well as the advent of the Messiah and the resurrection of the dead. This type of detail, and misinterpretations of the other visions, under the prism of most Christian theologians, lead one to suppose that many things said by Daniel still have to happen. Although, although Daniel said things that could be the beginning of questions related to the end of this Aeon (era, century, age, cycle, stage), the thesis of his comments must be complemented in light of history and other prophecies.

I. THE VISION OF THE STATUE

There are key historical visions seen by the prophet Daniel that deal with the past, even though many Christian theologians are convinced that they see quite a few descriptions of things yet to take place. There are indeed isolated comments on future things, where he directly interprets other people's dreams, or he is told by an angel. Since all this is usually separated by its corresponding chapter and consists of precise ideas, I will define it all as "visions" of his.

The first of these momentous revelations is seen by Nebuchadnezzar, but it is divinely made known to Daniel later to explain it to this king and to convince him of the power of God through the gift of revelation and interpretation given to Daniel. This subject is already dealt with in chapter 2 of his book, where Daniel describes a statue composed of various materials in sections, and which is understood to represent the kingdoms of Babylon (gold), Persia and Media (silver), Greece - Macedonia - (bronze), Rome (iron) and a mysterious 5th (iron and clay). That statue is knocked down by a stone cut and thrown by divine work, which crumbles the entire effigy. That stone is the coming kingdom of the Messiah and this is how the manuscript exposes:

« You, king, saw in your dream a great image. This image was very great and its glory, very sublime. He was standing before you and his appearance was terrible. The head of this image was of fine gold; his chest and arms of silver; his belly and his thighs, of bronze; his legs, of iron; his feet, partly of iron and partly of baked clay. You were looking, until a stone fell without any hand cutting it, and struck the image on its feet of iron and baked clay, and crushed them. Then the iron, the clay, the bronze, the silver, and the gold were also crushed to pieces, and they were like chaff from the summer threshing floors, and the wind carried them away without any trace of them remaining. But the stone that struck the image became a

great mountain that filled the whole earth ." (vers. 31-35. Translation of Reina Valera 1995)

The interpretation that Daniel refers to that king begins by clarifying: « *You are that head of gold.* » And adds:

« *After you another kingdom will arise, inferior to yours; and then a third kingdom of bronze, which will rule over all the earth. And the fourth kingdom will be strong as iron; and as iron crushes and breaks all things, so he will crush and break everything. What you saw of the feet and fingers, partly potter's clay and partly iron, will be a divided kingdom; but there will be in it something of the strength of iron, just as you saw iron mixed with clay. And because our toes are partly iron and partly clay, this kingdom will be partly strong and partly fragile. Just as you saw iron mixed with clay, so they will be mixed through human alliances; but they will not unite with each other, as iron does not mix with clay. In the days of these kings, the God of heaven will raise up a kingdom that will never be destroyed, nor will the kingdom be left to another people; He will crush and consume all these kingdoms, but he will remain forever, just as you saw that a stone fell from the mountain without any hand cutting it, and it crushed the iron, the bronze, the clay, the silver, and the gold. . The great God has shown the king what is to take place in the future; and the dream is true, and its interpretation faithful.*" (Vers. 38-45, RVA 95)

As in many other prophecies, it is understood that the roots of the "New World Order" (a global government) arise from Rome, which does not at all appear to be related to Rome but to the current powers and the UN. The 10 toes of the feet can precisely be understood as the same 10 horns of the beast of the vision of chapter 7, and of which the apostle John would also speak in Revelation. If we assume that the kingdom of the Messiah is established with the fall of this 5th kingdom, and the 5 are a block, where are all the geographical, governmental and political differences of the world? It is evident that from the 4th kingdom (Rome) an empire based on alliances is created, which are mixed and at the same time do not mix. If iron symbolizes

Rome, it is notorious that the feet of baked clay and iron are the combination of Roman power and other powers, but to a large extent they are not authentic alliances or are not bona fide. It's like an incombinable combination. Why then are they trying to unite? Is there something in common between them, an interest stronger than their own ideals, principles or ideology? This seems to be answered only by comparing it to Revelation:

« The ten horns that you have seen are ten kings who have not yet received a kingdom; but they will receive authority as kings for one hour, together with the beast. These <u>*have the same purpose*</u> *: they will give their power and authority to the beast .»* (Revelation 17:12-13, RVA 95)

As can be seen, as the empires pass, the quality of the material that symbolically composes them is lower, it even goes from minerals to the mud itself. What does the mud symbolize? The minerals are already molten, so these empires rise up with war, but the latter tries to combine what is "already made" with what is configured by man himself. Therefore, the interpretation of this would be the same as that of the rest of the apocalyptic quotes that describe a global government. The apostle John was told of a beast that had 7 heads, and that these heads represented 7 mountains, and in turn 7 kingdoms. Then they explain to him that 5 had already passed, that another "was", and that a last one would come before the advent of the Messiah to establish his kingdom. In John's time, the empire was Rome, once again coinciding with the aforementioned question, so if one assumes who the previous 5 would be, Babylon, Medo-Persia and Greece would clearly enter, as 3 of them, but, what and the other 2? Egypt and Assyria? And why in the other visions is it not told before about them? Possibly because Egypt was the first great empire of the known era of mankind since this aeon began counting, which may have coincided with the flood, and had nothing to do with the nation of Israel. From the flood to Egypt there was no power on Earth to be considered an empire, even though before Egypt there was a very close first attempt to achieve this with the "New York" of that time: the city of the tower of Babel.

« *When the great tower fell and the languages of men were separated to many languages of mortals, first was the royal power of Egypt established, that of the Persians and the Medes and also of the Ethiopians and of Assyria and Babylon. Then the great pride of Macedonia boasts, then, fifth, the famous last lawless kingdom of the Italians manifests many evils to all mortals and will have to endure the fatigues of men from all countries. And he will drive the kings of the untamed nations to the West, [to] make laws for the peoples and subdue all things .*" (Sibylline Oracles. Book VIII. Vers. 5-15)

This quote from the sibyl is very interesting, because it is one of several that supports the historical facts that most are unaware of, regarding how Rome transmuted into the US, first out of its desire to stifle Protestant influence, and eventually coming to all the seats of the legislative power, to the point of controlling the UN - evidently without any label that could relate it to Rome (of this it is necessary to know a lot about history, especially about the Jesuits and the founding of the USA) -. This is even more acceptable considering that Revelation describes a prostitute who defines Babel as 'Great Babylon', and who is set on fire by the very 10 kings of the beast on which she sat. It all started from the tower of Babel and it all ends with the burning of the latter Babel (a word that is transcribed into Greek as 'Babylon'). Now, in the count the number of empires differs here with respect to the influence in the times of the Hebrews - as I said a moment ago - since the Egyptian empire was prior to the Hebrews - regarding the context of what is being talked about (since the Egyptians, after the departure of the Hebrews, were not exactly a power opposed to the Hebrews, and progressively their strength began to wane alongside the Assyrian power) - and the Ethiopian did not influence Hebrew history or the rest of the world. world (possibly in the case of the kingdom of Aksum).

Consequently, Rome is defined as the 6th of the 7 heads of the beast that John saw, and of which he speaks in the 17th chapter of Revelation. But what is the 7th head? It is common in the various dogmas established by man that theses pointing to the opposite emerge here, saying that all this has already happened: an especially Catholic argument, to legitimize his 'Temporary Power', and exonerate himself from his part in this. But who destroys this empire? Not human hand, but the Messiah when he returns and establishes his kingdom, for he writes that " *the stone that struck the image **became a great mountain that filled the whole earth** *." (Dan. 2:35, R95), and adds that « *In the days of these kings, **the God of heaven will raise up a kingdom that will never be destroyed** , nor will the kingdom be left to another people; He will crush and consume all these kingdoms, but he will remain forever, just as you saw that a stone fell from the mountain without any hand cutting it, and it crushed the iron, the bronze, the clay, the silver and the gold. . The great God has shown the king what is to come in the future ...*» (Dan. 2:44-45, R95) Whose kingdom will this be but that of King Jesus Christ? Has that kingdom been established? The defenders of the 'Kingdom Now' would say that it is so, but compared to the last quotes of Revelation it is not like that at all: a millennium of peace has not begun, we do not have immortality, we do not have eternal life, Yeshua (Jesus) does not has not been manifested, neither has the Ancient of Days, there has been no resurrection of the dead, etc. Let us now compare these 7 empires defined by John, the 5 described by the Greek sibyl, and the 5 of the statue of Nebuchadnezzar with the 4 of the vision of Zacharias:

"*These are the horns that scattered Judah, Israel, and Jerusalem .*" (Ch. 1:19)

Who scattered Judah? First Babylon and finally Rome. Who scattered Israel? First Syria - although Israel was divided only as a nation - and what was left was exiled by the Romans (although the text does not say "take captive", but "scatter"). Who scattered Jerusalem? Babylon and Rome. We have here what appear to be Assyrians, Babylonians, and Romans. Another nation is missing, and from the context and meaning of the word 'Zarah', which also means to separate or waste, it is understood that the other could be Greece. What seems more than clear is that these visions speak of the empires that have preceded us, but they all continue to speak of Rome and the end of a last kingdom in relation to it, directly or indirectly. However, it is strange that they spoke in the past tense - "*they dispersed*" -, since in the time of Zacharias the Roman Empire did not yet exist, the Greeks and the Persians had not yet risen, and the deportation to Babylon had not yet occurred. However, the translation is something else with respect to semantics, since in Hebrew it does not define something past but timeless, and consequently it could be an announcement of something already seen from the future.

If this was not enough, some time later another dream would intrigue Nebuchadnezzar, and he would know that turning to Daniel would solve the enigma of his dream. However, what this dream experience announced might not please the king, although for his experience it would be something necessary that he had to go through:

« *These were the visions in my head while I was in my bed: I seemed to see a tree in the middle of the earth, whose height was great. This tree grew, and became strong, and its top reached the sky, and it could be seen from all ends of the earth. Its foliage was beautiful and its fruit abundant, and there was food for all in it. Under it the beasts of the field were placed in the shade, and in its branches the birds of the sky made their dwelling, and all flesh lived from it. I saw in the visions in my head while I was on my bed, that behold a watchful and holy one descended from heaven. And he cried out loudly and said thus: Tear down the tree, and cut off its branches, remove its foliage, and scatter its fruit; leave the beasts that are under it, and the birds from its branches. But the stump of its roots you will leave in the earth, with a bond of iron and bronze among the grass of the field; be wet with the dew of heaven, and with the beasts be their part among the grass of the earth. Let his heart be changed from a man, and the heart of a beast be given to him, and seven times pass over him. The sentence is by decree of the watchmen, and by the saying of the saints the resolution, so that the living may know that the Most High governs the kingdom of men, and that he gives it to whomever he wants, and establishes over it the lowest of men. the men .»* (Dan. 4:10-17, R60)

Daniel's subsequent interpretation turns out to be completely accurate, and everything he warns him about takes place, since it was something that was to happen to the king, but the beginning of what Nebuchadnezzar saw was basically the glory of his kingdom and the power acquired by his empire:

" The tree that you saw, which grew and became strong, and whose crown reached to the sky, and which could be seen from all the ends of the earth, whose foliage was beautiful, and its fruit abundant, and in which there was food for all , under whom the beasts of the field dwelt, and in whose branches the birds of the sky nested, you yourself are, O king, who grew and became strong, for your greatness increased and reached to the heavens, and your dominion to the heavens. ends of the earth ." (Dan. 4:20-22, R60)

However, this ruler of the Chaldean dynasty, having seen and experienced such rise and dominance, did not give God true honor, and was broken for a time:

« And as for what the king saw, a watcher and saint who descended from heaven and said: Cut down the tree and destroy it; but the stump of its roots you will leave in the earth, with a band of iron and bronze in the grass of the field; and let him be wet with the dew of heaven, and his part be with the beasts of the field, until seven times pass over him; This is the interpretation, O king, and the sentence of the Most High, which has come upon my lord the king: That they will drive you out from among men, and your dwelling shall be with the beasts of the field, and they will feed you with the grass of the field like animals. the oxen, and with the dew of the sky you will be bathed; and seven times will pass over you, until

you know that the Most High has dominion in the kingdom of men, and that he gives it to whomever he wants. And as for the order to leave the stump of the roots of the same tree on earth, it means that your kingdom will remain firm after you recognize that heaven rules. Therefore, oh king, accept my advice: redeem your sins with justice, and your iniquities by showing mercy to the oppressed, for perhaps that will be an extension of your peace of mind. All this came upon King Nebuchadnezzar." (Dan. 4:23-28, R60)

II. THE VISION OF THE FOUR BEASTS

After the important place that Daniel acquires in the court of King Nebuchadnezzar, several years seem to pass, in which certain experiences dignify him as an example of faith and strength, but at a certain moment the theme of the visions is mentioned again. First, he anticipates a state of madness for the king into which he would enter due to his vainglory (chapter 4) and in what seems to be decades later he himself is the one who begins to see things for a future further away in time, not without first noticing to the succession of the king that they would be subdued by the Persians and their dynasty would end (cap. 5). At some point, between this predicted end to glorious Babylon and its taking by Cyrus the Great, Daniel is anticipated what would happen thereafter to define the final guidelines of time for mankind. , just before its outcome and the beginning of an era of light. In chapter 7 of his book, Daniel 7 speaks of four beasts, saying:

« *I looked in my vision at night, and I saw that the four winds of the sky fought in the great sea. And four great beasts, different one from the other, came up out of the sea. The first was like a lion, and had eagle's wings. I was watching until its wings were torn off; she was lifted up from the ground and stood on her feet like a man, and a man's heart was given to her. Then I saw a second beast, like a bear, which stood taller on one side than the other. In his mouth, between his teeth, he had three ribs; and it was said to him: "Rise and devour much meat." After this I looked, and another, similar to a leopard, with four wings of a bird on its back. This beast had four heads; and he was given dominion. After this I looked in the visions of the night, and I saw the fourth beast ...*» (Vers. 2-7, R95)

When speaking of " *the four winds of heaven* " , he refers to the 4 cardinal points, that is, he describes a large-scale conflict, not a simple local or national war. The idea of "great sea" may be a reference to the open sea, since the Hebrews also called the great lakes a sea, such as the Sea of Tiberias or Galilee, or the Red Sea, or it may be a reference to the Mediterranean Sea. Others might go beyond this elementary interpretation and assume that the vision emphasizes that what it is about to speak of is reflected in a celestial conflict. Now, if we analyze this vision in the light of the Oahspe, it would seem to indicate that the world suffers a religious war from then until the present, but following a chronological sequence of history, and comparing it with other visions, we find it obvious that it mentions the 4 great empires from that time to the present: 1st Babylon, 2nd Media-Persia, 3rd Macedonia and 4th Rome. From the 4th would emerge the final estate with its 10 horns, that is, it would be the global government, from where Belial (the false prophet) emerges.

Babylon and the symbol of the winged lion are very appropriate, as is the vision of King Nebuchadnezzar being first humbled and then dignified because of his understanding, when God had to break his pride. Then Persia as a bear, and that it is leaning more on one side than the other while having 3 ribs in its teeth, could be an indication of 3 very important kingdoms that it wiped out in its path. Being more loaded on one side than the other could be a matter related to their imperial administration system. However, the one that seems even clearer is the 3rd of these beasts, which due to its feline characteristics, be it leopard or tiger, it is evident that it expanded rapidly. Relating its 4 wings with the 4 ends of the world, we find more analogies with the rest of the prophecies and sources that speak of Greece. Just as the great Persian leaders were called "King of the World" and "King of the four corners of the Earth", the rise of Alexander the Great would be the embodiment of this idea, extending his empire to the 4 cardinal points. Then, those 4 heads would be the 4 generals that succeed him after his death.

« *After this I looked in the visions of the night, and I saw the fourth beast, frightful, terrible and in a great way strong, which had great iron* *teeth; she devoured and crumbled, trampled the scraps under her feet, and was very different from all the beasts she had seen before her; and **it had ten horns** . While I was contemplating the horns, **another little horn came up among them** , and three of the first horns were plucked up before it. This horn had eyes like a man and a mouth that spoke with great insolence. I watched until **some thrones were set up and an Ancient of days sat down** . Her dress was white as snow; the hair of his head, like clean wool; his throne, a flame of fire, and burning fire its wheels. A river of fire came and went from before him; thousands upon thousands served him, and millions upon millions were before him. The Judge sat down and the books were opened. I then watched because of the sound of the great insolences that the horn spoke; and **while he looked they killed the beast, and its body was torn to pieces and given up to be burned in the fire** ."* (Dan. 7:7-11)

It should be noted that in addition to the fact that this is designated as the last kingdom that would exist on Earth - that is, until the coming of the Lord -, it contains clear components that associate it with the beast defined by the apostle John in Revelation 17:

*"... and I saw a woman sitting on a scarlet beast full of blasphemous names, having seven heads and ten horns. [...] on her forehead a name written, a mystery: BABYLON THE GREAT, THE MOTHER OF HARLOTS AND OF THE ABOMINATIONS OF THE EARTH. [...] The beast that you have seen was, and is not; and it is about to rise from the abyss and go to perdition; and the inhabitants of the earth, those whose names are not written from the foundation of the world in the book of life, will be astonished seeing the beast that was and is not, and will be. [...] This, for the mind that has wisdom: The seven heads are seven mountains, on which the woman sits, and they are seven kings. Five of them have fallen; one is, and the other has not yet come; and when it comes, it must last a short time. The beast that was, and is not, **is also the eighth** ; and **he is among the seven**, and goes to perdition. And the ten horns that you have seen are ten kings, who have not yet received a kingdom; but for one hour*

they will receive authority as kings together with the beast. These have the same purpose, and they will give their power and their authority to the beast. They will fight against the Lamb, and the Lamb will overcome them, for he is Lord of lords and King of kings; and those who are with him are called and chosen and faithful. [...] And the ten horns that you saw on the beast, these will hate the harlot, and will leave her desolate and naked; and they will devour its flesh, and burn it with fire; because God has put in their hearts to execute what he wanted: agree, and give his kingdom to the beast, until the words of God are fulfilled. And the woman you have seen is the great city that reigns over the kings of the earth. » (vers. 3-18, R60)

Some are of the opinion that this beast bears no relation to the one Daniel saw, even despite the clear parallels. One of the arguments to support this is that the 4th beast that Daniel spoke of was not described as having 7 heads. Although, this could be justified considering that Daniel's vision spoke of the 4 great empires from the days of Daniel until the coming of the Messiah, while John's only focused on the details of this last power. That would explain why they tell John that the beast is also from among the 7, and is also the 8th: if the 6th was Rome, and another was to ascend (the 7th), this seems to be a government established based on the 6th. (Rome), but in addition to being a 7th empire, or the "global government", it is itself a ruler and possibly a government as well. It's very simple, if the 10 leaders were the 10 most powerful individuals in the world today, and they pass their power to the beast, who is the beast? If it is a government, someone must be the head of the government, and if it is the head of a government, where is that government located? But those who think this is different from Daniel's also stick to the fact that Daniel mentions an 11th character who will emerge and take down 3 of the 10, which Revelation says nothing about:

« The fourth beast will be a fourth kingdom on the earth, which will be different from all the other kingdoms, and will devour the whole earth,

*thresh it and tear it to pieces. The ten horns mean that ten kings will arise from that kingdom; and **after them another will rise**, which will be different from the first, and will overthrow three kings. He will speak words against the Most High, he will break the saints of the Most High, and he will think of changing the times and the Law; and they will be delivered into his hands until a time, times and half a time. **But the Judge will sit, and his dominion will be taken away**, so that it will be destroyed and ruined to the end, **and that the kingdom, the dominion and the majesty of the kingdoms under all heaven will be given to the people of the saints of the Most High**, whose kingdom is an everlasting kingdom, and **all dominions will serve and obey him**."* (Dan. 7:23-27, RVA 95)

At this point Daniel and Juan have more successes in common than discrepancies, and it is notorious that both speak of a character that will emerge at the last moment, when the beast has received the power of these 10 "lords" or sovereigns. Both agree that when this arrives, the end of said government will also come, and it will come with the advent of the Messiah and a delegate of God. These things were revealed to God's servants after Daniel:

*« Then I saw a dream, and behold, an eagle came from the sea, having twelve feathered wings, and three heads. [...] And I saw that all things under heaven were subject to it, and none spoke against it, no, not to a creature on earth. [...] But **the heads will be kept for the last**. [...] Then [the] head a voice that said to me: Look before you, and consider what you see. And I looked, and behold, as if it were **a roaring lion**, **emerging from the tree**, and I saw that he sent a man's voice to the eagle, and said to him: listen, I am going to speak with you, and the Most High says to you, **Are you not the one who remains of the four beasts**, who reigns in my world, who at the end of his time can come through them? And **the fourth came, and surpassed all the beasts that had passed**, and had power over the world, with great fear, and over all the bubble of the earth*

with much wicked oppression, and <u>thus long lived on the earth with deceit</u> ... ." (2 Ezra 11)

Here Ezra confirms that the 4th beast will be the last, and that it will be judged directly by the Messiah, when the Lord returns, and also confirms that this beast is the only one that would remain until the end. Then, they add the rest of the information to the scribe:

« Because you have judged me worthy, show me the last times. And he said to me: This is the interpretation of the vision: **The eagle, which you have seen coming from the sea, is the kingdom that was seen in the vision of your brother Daniel** . *However, it was not explained to him, therefore I will now declare it to you. Behold, the day will come, that* **a kingdom will rise up on the earth, and it will be feared above all the kingdoms that were before it** . *[...] And the lion, whom you have seen, coming up from the wood, and roaring, and spoke with the eagle, and [him] rebuked for his injustice with all the words that you have heard; This is* **<u>the anointed</u>** , *whom the Most High <u>has reserved for them and for their wickedness to the end</u> : let them be rebuked, and rebuke them with their cruelty ."* (2 Ezra 12)

In addition to Ezra, at least 100 years earlier Baruch had also been informed of this issue:

« And he answered and said to me: Baruch, this is the interpretation of the vision that you have seen. [...] Behold the days to come, and <u>this kingdom will be destroyed once it destroyed Zion</u> , and **it will be subjected to the one that comes after** . *On the other hand, that also <u>after a time it will be destroyed</u> , and another,* **a third, will be produced, and that it will also have dominion over its time, and they will be destroyed** . *And after these things <u>[a] fourth kingdom will come into being, whose power will be harsh and evil far beyond those that were before it</u> , [...] And because the truth is hidden, and all those who are defiled with iniquity to flee with him, [...] which will come to pass* **when the moment of its consummation which has been directed to fall, then the Principality of My Messiah will be revealed** , *which is like the fountain and the vine,*

and when it becomes manifest to root of the multitude of his host ..." (2nd Baruch 39)

The characteristic of lies and deceit is quite representative of current power, ranging from Rome to the current shadow power, what some call the Illuminati. Here we observe that Baruch was also told about these kingdoms, starting with Babylon, who in his time had "destroyed Zion", and therefore they would also be destroyed. If we remember, Baruch was a scribe of the prophet Jeremiah, and both witnessed the destruction of Jerusalem and the First Temple by Babylonian power. After this empire he was told that one would come who would "subdue" Babylon, which corresponds with the Persians, and then this, in turn, would also be destroyed after a while. Another would come and have dominion in his time before also being destroyed, and it is necessary to remember that Greece defeated Persia "after a while", since at first the Hellenes were subdued by the Medo-Persians. If the third were the Hellenes, the reference is just as apt: Alexander took revenge on the Persians long after they had dominated the Greeks. Later we see that he speaks again of the 4th kingdom, and which reaches its consummation when the principality or reign of the Messiah begins to be revealed, that is, the signs begin to begin its establishment.

" For before the companions of Alexander, king of Macedonia, who lived comparatively a short time ago, the sea of Pamphylia receded and made way for them, when they had no other way to go, and that was when it was the will of God to destroy **the Persian monarchy** *. <u>The fact is recognized as authentic by all who have written about the actions of Alexander</u> ."* (Antiquities of the Jews. Book I. Cap. XVI, vers. 5. Tito Flavio Josefo)

Regarding the last horn that Daniel mentions, saying that it comes after the 10, he affirms that *" it will be different from the first ones "*, although he does not specify in what way. If we suppose that these 10 are kings, how do we fit this version with today? Yes, there are basically 10 monarchies in Europe, but, as far as is known, they do not in sum even represent the greatest wealth or power in the world, except for the

Danish and British houses. If they were the 10 FEMA generals, that would only apply to the US, not the rest of the world. If it were 10 named leaders, I could support the theory of the world being divided into 10 sections, something like in 'The Hunger Wars', but if so we would still have to see the consequential changes to bring you to that situation . Despite this, considering 10 individuals "named" is a rare democratic idea in the "enlightenment", and given a group of families that control the entire planet, why would they name 10 people? Why not 8 or 12, or 15? What if we are talking about the 10 most powerful people in the world? Apocalypse says that they will receive power in one hour together with the beast, and that suggests whether then they would be chosen characters, or they themselves, by autocracy or by influence over the people, be defined as the legitimate rulers who are to direct the planet.

Will they receive power in an hour? The "hour" in the Hebrew language is a linguistic generality used as in other languages, both for 60 minutes and for a specific "moment". Like when we say " *this is the right time* " or " *it's lunchtime* ", referring to a short time frame, not necessarily 60 minutes. Be that as it may, after these leaders or "masters" comes another that is different, and if it is different, it may be that it does not necessarily belong to a royal caste, a wealthy mafia, a government monopoly, a political union or things of that nature. It is said of him that " *He will speak words against the Most High* ", something that is similar to what was said by John, either regarding the false prophet or the 8th, that is, the beast itself:

« *He was also given a mouth that spoke great things and blasphemies; and he was given authority to act for forty-two months. And he opened his mouth in blasphemies against God, to blaspheme his name, his tabernacle, and those who dwell in heaven .*" (Rev. 13:5-6, R60)

Interesting coincidence with Daniel:

«*... after them another will rise, which will be different from the first, and will overthrow three kings. He will speak words against the Most High,* *he will break the saints of the Most High, and he will think of changing the times and the Law; and they will be delivered into his hands until a time, times and half a time. But the Judge will sit, and his dominion will be taken away ..."* (Dan. 7:24-26, R95)

Baruch also talks about this topic and refers to the fact that said individual will remain until the last moment, to be judged in the presence of the Messiah:

« *<u>The last leader of that moment will be left alive</u>*, **when the multitude of his troops will put themselves to the sword**, and **<u>he will be subdued, and they will take him to Mount Zion, and my Messiah will condemn him for all his impieties</u>**, *and they will gather before him. him and establish all the works of his hosts. And afterwards, he will be put to death, and [will] protect the rest of my people who are in the place I have chosen. And the Principality will be forever, until the world of corruption is at an end, and until the established deadlines are met. This is his vision, and this is his interpretation*." (2nd Baruch 40)

Clearly this is the same example and the same parameter that the visions of Daniel and John follow in their Apocalypse:

« *I saw the beast and the kings of the earth and their armies, gathered together to make war against him who sat on the horse and against his army. The beast was caught, and with it the false prophet...* » (Rev. 19:19-20, RVA 95)

How is it that the horn defeats the saints? Revelation also speaks of this, referring to the situation of those servants of God who are left behind after the Rapture, symbolically narrating that " *the dragon was filled with anger against the woman; and he went to make war against the rest of her offspring, those who keep the commandments of God and have the testimony of Jesus Christ* ." (Rev. 12:17, R60). In addition to that, other sources confirm that the Messiah will return together with a personification of God (called 'Ancient of Days' or 'Head of Days'), which in turn is a figure of Yeshua's own father (Jesus):

*« I asked the angel who was with me and who showed me all the secret things regarding this **Son of Man** : "Who is this, where does he come from and **why does he go with the Head of Days** ?". He answered me and said: This is the Son of Man, who possesses justice and with whom justice lives and who will reveal all the hidden treasures, because the Lord of spirits has chosen him and his destiny is the greatest dignity before the Lord. of the spirits, justly and forever. The Son of Man whom you have seen will raise up kings and mighty ones from their beds and the mighty from their thrones; **he will loosen the bridles of the strong and break the teeth of sinners** ; <u>He will overthrow kings from their thrones and kingdoms</u>, because they have not exalted and praised him or humbly acknowledged where kingship was bestowed on them. It will change the face of the strong, filling them with fear; darkness will be their home and worms their bed, and they will have no hope of getting up from that bed, because they have not exalted the name of the Lord of spirits . »* (2nd Enoch 46:2-6)

We can conclude that this portion of the book of Daniel really tells us about past and future episodes, but are there more parts where Daniel also talks about future things? We have that the 1st beast is Babylon, the second is Persia, the third is Greece and the fourth is Rome. Some have refuted that Greece does not enter here , even saying that it did not exist until the 19th century; logically it is a misplaced argument. That region was under Ottoman occupation until the wars of independence in which Russia, France and England helped them, but that did not mean that it ceased to be historically Greece, or before that the Hellenes or Ionians. The Second Beast (Persia-Media) invaded the Hellenic peoples starting with Thermopylae, that is, the Spartan stronghold. We know that at that time the Greeks (whose term comes from Graikos, a son of Zeus and Pandora), were a series of feuding peoples that not even Agamemnon could perfectly organize to take the 7th Troy (13th century BC), but After the bravery of the Spartans, many Hellenic peoples (name derived from the ancient inhabitants of Hellas) joined, despite the many lost battles. Years later, Alexander the

Great wanted revenge and subdued the Persians and reached India. He died in his bed, and Seleucus, Ptolemy, Cassander and Lysimachus took power in each of the 4 regions (Daniel 8:8 and 21-22) to which the empire had extended and maintained Hellenic-Greek power until the rise the Roman Empire.

It is interesting to observe that Daniel warns about the advent of the Antichrist (called 'Belial'), and despite this, many believe that it is not a reference to it, and not only that, but even if it were, there are no more allusions – for not say that none except in Revelation - that speaks of said individual. On the contrary, this being is mentioned in many sources:

A – 'The Wars of the Sons of Light against the Sons of Darkness', from the Qumran manuscripts, points to the Antichrist – either directly or spiritually – militarily supporting the Romans (the 4th beast).

B – '2nd Thessalonians 2', where Paul mentions that Satan will be behind the manifestation of this individual; that the Iniquitous will perform false miracles, stand on the Holy Place and also impose himself against all sacred things.

C – 'Gospel of Ammonius', where it is explained that the Eschatological Sermon was an announcement of the events that will precede the manifestation of the Antichrist.

D – 'Apocalypse of Elijah', where the prophet points out that the Antichrist will appear just before the Messiah in his glorious coming, and will deceive the world with false miracles.

E – 'The Ascension of Isaiah', where the prophet announces the coming of the Antichrist, how he will lead many away from the faith, how he will place his image before him in every city, how long he will exercise power, how it will end, etc.

F – 'Gospel of Nicodemus', where Enoch and Elijah announce their return to preach in Jerusalem against the Antichrist, and to be killed at 3 and a half years of age, but to be resurrected on the third day and taken back to heaven.

G – 'Apocalypse of Thomas' reiterates that the Eschatological Sermon (world war, famine, epidemics and earthquakes followed by signs from heaven) announced the manifestation of the Antichrist.

H – 'Secret Book of John' and '2nd Treaty of Set' relate the origin of Belial.

I – 'The Major Keys of Solomon' refer that the Antichrist will come to establish a temporary kingdom with the return of Enoch and Elijah, and after these three the Messiah will appear.

As for the apostle Paul, he tells us about two keys to come before the return of Christ: apostasy and the antichrist. The first must come for the second to be manifested, and then the wrath of God comes. The spirit of truth must be eliminated from the whole world (although we remain a few minorities) so that the other spirit, that of the antichrist, can manifest itself. I am not going to go into emphasis on history or give a lecture on the progress of Rome and the founding of the USA, because I have already dealt with that in previous works, but for those of us who study history we know that Rome (the 4th beast) it has changed its facade and strategies from the beginning, and used the rise of the US to continue from there to control the world, so that the Vatican was not identified as the source of power and influence. All the power of Rome, through the Jesuits, passed to the entire estate of the US over the course of more than two centuries. The Bible neither says this nor does it stop saying it, empirically, because the Bible finished developing in a historical period that ended in the first century AD. C. (16 centuries before the appearance of the USA).

The beast brings apostasy, so that the beast itself can rise up without opposition, that is, this is the spirit of the antichrist. Antichrist is to oppose everything that has to do with the figure of Christ, and apostasy is to deny the customs, beliefs and religious or cultural-ancestral traditions. The combination of both things is precisely the gateway to the Great Tribulation. Apostasy is being seen tremendously in popular culture and in religious sects (sects, or groups, denominations, etc.) that are turning to fables, spirits of deceit, fanaticism, liberality, debauchery, degradation, etc. The spirit of the antichrist is also moving at the social level, especially in laws and jurisprudence that is taking away the role of Christianity and, on the contrary, is giving rise to public satanism, social degradation, child sexual perversion in schools, etc.

III. COULD THE BEAST BE ISLAM?

Among the many eschatological theories and theses that exist, there is a recent one that has become popular among certain people and religious groups, and it is the one that believes that the Beast is Islam itself. Supporters of this new trend claim that Revelation 13:18 originally mentioned the name 'Allah', but still in Greek it says 'arithmos' ("number"), not "name". That is, it is written « *the number is ...* » , not "the name is...". There, in particular, he is talking about a number, not a name, which usually coincides with the "Christian Kabbalah", to call it that, where the Christians used methods already known among the Jews, in which using the value of the letters they coded a name. For example, if the Hebrew word 'Aba' (Father) were a proper name, the value of its letters would be 4 (A = 1 + B = 2 + A = 1).

Now, the way in which Allah is written in Arabic bears no resemblance to the order of Ji-Chi-Stigma, which are the original characters found in Greek manuscripts. Not even in the Arabic Bible, like the Van Dyke version, characters appear with any kind of similarity between the two concepts. In addition to this, the letters ji-chi-stigma cannot be pronounced because they do not have vowels, except as "jxs" or "jhchs", which more than Greek would seem like some alien language. In itself, Allah in Greek is 'Alláx' (Alfa-Lamda-Lamda-Alfa-Ji), and is pronounced 'Aláj'. But those who believe in this thesis maintain that the spelling of Islam, Daesh and Allah are all linked and associated with the name and number of the beast, also arguing that the final sound of 'Allah', as seen in Spanish, would be hidden in the Greek form of the letter Sigma. To begin with, it would be absurd to assume that they added a "tilde", this being merely a matter of Spanish, and with regard to the equality of the characters themselves - in my opinion - they do not even resemble each other. Just the 'Chi', looking vertical and then horizontal would seem to be part of the structure of the name Allah, but to my mind that's not proof of anything but chance mixed with a desire to force an image into the shape it's intended to be. you want me to have. For example, the verse of Apoc. 13:18 does not say that "it is the number of a man " , but that " the number " of Thíriou " *is the number of a man* " , that is, of a person (even that cannot be interpreted as "number of a deity" , as is the chaos of Allah).

In itself it is somewhat absurd to associate Arabic with the writing of the Apocalypse. In the time of the Apostle John - 500 years before Muhammad - the Arabs called God 'Allah Tohalla', and if John - who is not known to know Arabic - had wanted to write 'Allah Tohalla', or just 'Allah ', would have violated his own faith, because Allah is just the Arabic translation for God. In the worst case, it would have written "islam", or even more concise and direct words, such as "sharia", "shii" or "daesh". Although, those who follow this current even define the Arabic word 'Allah' as a "blasphemous name". The Greek word 'God' that is used so much worldwide in every language and translation is an epithet of the Greek deity Zeus, from the root 'Day' (daylight), that is to say "the one who provides the light". Just as 'god' is translated in Hebrew as 'Eloah' (hence the plural "elohim"), in Arabic its equivalent is 'Allah' or 'Allah'. What's blasphemy about that? The root of Elh (Eloah) is 'El', and is the same Semitic cognate of 'Alh' (Allah). If the one is blasphemous, is not the other? In addition to this, these people maintain that the name of Allah appears in Revelation as "two crossed swords", but no matter how much I have analyzed the name 'Allah' I have not found it, nor what they pretend to see, I conclude that Allah would be the equivalent from Castilian "God".

The word 'God', in Greek, is Theos, hence the relationship with Zeus (the one who has life), in English it is God, from the German Gott, and this in turn from Wott, and that from the Scandinavian Wottan (the form more common to call Odin). In Chinese it is Shen and in Japanese it is Kami; in Russian it is Bog and in French it is Dieu. As with the Greek Theos, Dieu became God, and these all come from the Sanskrit Djaus (giving rise to 'Zeus'), which was part of the full name Djauspitar (returning to Roman 'Jupiter), the name of god in ancient India (before the cult of Brahma), and where 'Diaush-Pitá' means "father of heaven". The Hebrew term 'Alah' has many connotations and meanings, ranging from swearing, imprecating, perjuring, cursing; oath; lament, sigh; not being able to do something despite trying; solemn warning; Holm oak; these; and in Aramaic 'God'. From the word 'Alah' comes the Hebrew 'Aloh' (the same term with the 'Vav' in the middle, which is pronounced 'Eloah' (God). The same in Arabic, where "God" is said 'Alah', because the Arabs do not speak Hebrew, nor Aramaic, nor Greek nor Spanish. There is this trend on the internet of translating 'biaism allah' (in the name of Allah) with characters supposedly similar to two crossed swords, a letter similar to the Greek 'chi' horizontally, and another character that makes it look like the Greek letter 'stigma'. They even take phrases from the jihadists to reconfigure them in such a way that they resemble this speculation as much as possible. All this is very forced, even who reads 'biasim allah in Arabic ' see that it has nothing to do with the idea that is fashionable among many now.

Among the things said by these theorists is that the mark of Cain and the mark of the beast are two completely different things. The "mark" of Cain, what is it? In Hebrew it says 'Aot' (letter, sign), which the Jews translated to the LXX as 'Simeion' (sign, sign). The "mark" of the beast, what is it? In Greek it says 'jaragma' which refers to an incision, a puncture in the skin, a wound; It is not something metaphorical or symbolic, but something that will be pricked in the skin and without which no one will be able to buy or sell. If they cannot compare or sell with that, they will want to prick people on the back of their hands, they are talking about the economy, a substitute for money, credit cards, checks, coins, that is, currencies . A type of digital or electronic currency, and unless the Arabs are construed to control the world economy, this assumption makes no sense. What's more, if the letters ji, chi and stigma are studied, they coincide with the 'jaragma', because Ji means 'life', Chi is the 'vital energy' that flows through our body, the fluctuations of the body's energy (which they use the human implantation chips to stay powered up), and Stigma is a wound on the skin (hence the word "stigma").

There is much more to this thesis, but it falls under its own weight, like the idea of the 7 mountains of the beast, which they claim are Arabian seas. The last straw, because Arabia does not border the Mediterranean, nor the Caspian, nor the Negro. The Gulfs of Aden and Oman are not seas but gulfs, and belong to the Arabian Sea (Arabian Sea) in the Indian Ocean. Arabia only has a sea on its right in the Persian "gulf", and on its left with the – indeed – sea, which is the reeds, or 'red'. The Gulf of Aden belongs to Somalia and Yemen, not Arabia. Arabia has no jurisdiction there, nor territory, nor in Oman. Well, leaving aside this curiosity that I wanted to add in that work, let's continue on the subject.

IV. VISION OF THE GOAT AND THE RAM

Following the order of the chapters of Daniel, and assuming that they have a writing order where he was going to note his experiences, we have that this prophet had another vision after the one of the 4 beasts. Two years had elapsed, according to him, when, while in Elam, he had another vision like the previous one, but in this case with two animals fighting. In his description, the first to appear is a ram, that is, an adult "male sheep":

« I lifted up my eyes and looked, and behold, a ram stood before the river, and it had two horns; and though the horns were high, one was higher than the other; and the tallest grew afterwards. I saw that the ram smote the west, north, and south with its horns, and that no beast could stop before it, nor was there anyone who escaped from its power; and he did according to his will, and magnified himself. While I was considering this, behold, a he-goat came from the west over the face of the whole earth, without touching the ground; and that he-goat had a remarkable horn between his eyes. » (Ch. 8:3-5, RVA 60)

Then in his experience the archangel Gabriel appears, who explains to him that the ram *« that had two horns, these are the kings of Media and Persia. The goat is the king of Greece, and the great horn that was between his eyes is the first king ."* (Vers. 20-21) However, in those days Belshazzar, son of King Nabonidus and the last of Babylon, ruled (although it would seem that Daniel implies that Belshazzar was the direct son of Nebuchadnezzar), so the end of the age was anticipated for him. brilliant Babylonian empire, being followed by the power of two emerging kingdoms that would clash with each other. Persia, Media and Greece were already known kingdoms, and especially Greece in a very distant time had been a great nation (or coalition of peoples of great splendor), but now Daniel was anticipated that they would rise up and contend in a terrible way. , and their war would change the world at that time. The fight between the goat (Greece) and the ram (Persia) is basically the medical wars:

« *And he came up to the two-horned ram, which I had seen on the river bank, and ran against him with the fury of his might. And I saw him come near the ram, and he rose up against him and struck him, and broke both of his horns, and the ram had not strength to stand before him; therefore he struck it down to the ground, and trampled it down, and there was no one to deliver the ram out of his power. And the goat grew exceedingly great; but when it was at its greatest strength, that great horn was broken, and in its place came forth four other notable horns toward the four winds of heaven .*" (Verses 6-8)

We know from history that the Persians invaded Greece from Ionia (547 BC), crossing the Hellespont and through Thrace into Macedonia, but meeting the brake of the Spartan army at Thermopylae, to protect the Aegean and the most important cities of the Hellenes. The Greeks were defeated and had to submit to the Persians, but their growing resentment led to new uprisings against the invaders from 499 BC. C. Thus, for 490 a. C. the great wars were unleashed that would lead to the complete capture of Greece by the Persians in 478 a. C. However, Daniel's vision at this point does not emphasize this background, except to speak of the power of the ram. What he does begin to narrate is from the raising of the goat (Greece), whose notable horn that breaks the two of the ram is Alexander the Great. Although there were more conflicts after 478 a. C., like the campaigns of Xerxes, and that arrived at 429 a. C. With a peace treaty from the Persian king Artaxerxes I, Alexander, almost a century later (334 BC) began a tremendously fast and withering crusade against the Persians, crushing them and reaching India, only slowed down by his health.

« *Alexander of Macedonia, son of Philip, left the country of Chitim, and after defeating Darius, king of the Persians and the Medes, reigned in his place, first of all over Hellas. He fought many battles, conquered strongholds, and slew kings of the earth. He advanced to the ends of the world and plundered a multitude of nations. The earth was silent in his presence and for this reason his heart was haughty and filled with pride. He assembled a powerful army, and subdued provinces, nations, and dynasties, which paid him tribute. Then he fell ill and, realizing that he was going to die, he summoned his generals, the nobles who had been educated with him since his youth and, before his death, divided his kingdom among them. Alexander died after reigning twelve years, and his generals took over the government, each in his own region. As soon as he died, they all put on the crown, and their sons succeeded them for many years, filling the land with calamities .* » (1 Maccabees 1:1-9, Septuagint)

Chapter 8 could be said to begin by giving clear propaganda to Alexander, exalted by his enterprise, but " *being at his greatest strength* ", it turns out that " *he was broken* ", coming to be succeeded by his 4 generals, because " *in his place they left four other notable horns toward the four winds of heaven* ." This is not the only time that Daniel is anticipated these events, since later on other revelations let him know that after the Achaemenid power there would rise "later a *valiant king* " who would dominate " *with great power* " and who would do his will until when it would be broken and its power bequeathed to its 4 principals (Dan. 11:3-4). Who were those 4? Seleucus, Ptolemy, Cassander and Lysimachus, each regent of a region under Hellenic rule: Cassander dominated the north, which was basically Macedonia and Greece; Lysimachus, for his part, ruled next door, all of Thrace and the so-called Asia (what would currently be western Turkey); Ptolemy ruled the south, that is, Egypt, being specially mentioned in Daniel 11 because of the struggles between him and the Egyptian power; Cassander, from where comes that " *little horn* " that brings evil to the Hebrew people, ruled the east, the enormous expanse that went as far as Persia itself. The vision that Daniel narrates in chapter 8 of his book

is not limited to Alexander and his successors, but anticipates events by a descendant of one of his generals, which would affect the Jews:
" *And out of one of them came a little horn, which grew great toward the south, and toward the east, and toward the glorious land. And it was magnified to the host of heaven; and part of the host and of the stars he cast to the ground, and trampled them under foot. He even exalted himself against the prince of hosts, and for him the daily sacrifice was taken away, and the place of his sanctuary was thrown to the ground. And because of the prevarication the army was delivered to him together with the continuous sacrifice; and he cast down the truth, and did what he wanted, and prospered* ." (Dan. 8:6-12, RVA 60)
Daniel saw his vision coming from the "west" because he was "east": He had the vision not in Israel but in Elam. Alexander not only took revenge on the Persians, he took all the regions, such as Anatolia and Assyria, which are northern regions (although eastern, taking Macedonia as a reference), and Egypt, which are southern regions (south, east, and glorious land). In other words, the division led the "horn" to seize power over the entire empire that was historically Hellenic (east, Egypt, Greece, and even the provinces of Judeah). Saying, "four winds of heaven", instead of clarifying "north, south, east and west" means that it goes "in all directions", not being a strictly symmetrical movement, but a general one. For this reason it clarifies that the horn goes to the south, east and to the glorious land. Who then was that little horn? Antiochus Epiphanes (Antiochus IV). The definition 'Keren' (horn) is a symbolism for 'leader'. The euphemism for "little" is used for the age or official rank of the individual. Indeed the "little horn" of Daniel 7:8 is the son of iniquity, but the "little horn" of Daniel 8:9 was the end of Antiochus III and everything related to Antiochus Epiphanes, his son. The little horn of Daniel 7:8 is Antichrist, and the little horn of Daniel 8:9 is Antiochus Epiphanes. Clarifying that even the translation itself is already an interpretation, not something literal, we go to the historical aspect of each section.

Daniel 8:11-13 is narrating the war between the Greeks and the Medo-Persians in the midst of which Judea is also affected. In 323 B.C. C., Alexander (Alexander the Great) dies and power passes to his generals, among which Ptolemy and Seleucus stand out. Alexander got along with the Jews because of an embassy that had told him that it was prophesied by Daniel that he would go far, but he should not attack the Hebrew people. However, Antiochus IV Epiphanes (175 and 164 BC) suspended liturgical and religious activities in Judea, ceased continuous sacrifice and all kinds of spiritual affairs in the temple.

As Daniel prophesies, after several years the Jews restore religious activities, thanks to the wars raised by the Maccabean brothers (hammer), who restored the services, purified the temple, put oil and lamps again, renewed the sacrifices. This was so important to Hebrew history that to this day it is celebrated as one of the most important festivals in Judaism: Hanukkah (the festival of lights). Among other sources, this is recorded not only in the early books of the Maccabees, but also in the Talmud. There, among other descriptions that detail the matter, it clearly says that by order of Antiochus IV " *burnt offerings, sacrifices, and libations had to be suppressed in the Sanctuary .*" » (1st Mac. 1:45), after the massacres, looting, perversion and subjugation that caused treason. Now, it is known that the father of Antiochus Epiphanes, Antiochus III the Great, failed when he ran into the emerging Roman Empire. He was defeated twice, at Thermopylae (191 BC) and at the Battle of Magnesia in 190 BC. C., against the Roman general Lucio Cornelio Escipión, and three years later he died raising his son Seleuco IV Filopátor for a few years until his assassination, since Antiochus Epiphanes immediately took office. The Maccabees tell it like this:

« From them arose a wicked scion, Antiochus Epiphanes, son of King Antiochus, who had been a hostage in Rome and ascended the throne in the one hundred and thirty-seventh year of the Greek Empire. It was then that a group of renegades appeared in Israel who seduced many, saying:

"Let us make an alliance with the neighboring nations, because since we separated from them, many evils have befallen us." This proposal was well received, and some of the people went immediately to see the king and he gave them authorization to follow the customs of the pagans. They built a gymnasium in Jerusalem in the style of the pagans, they hid the mark of circumcision and, reneging on the holy alliance, they joined the pagans and gave themselves up to all kinds of evil. " (1st Mac. 1:10-15)

It is possible that Daniel was also told about this much later, as reflected in chapter 12 of his book, but focusing at this moment on the words referred to here, since there seem to be arguments to suppose that this could not be historically correct, but it's not like that. The " *trodden army* " of which the passage speaks, to whom does it belong? At first the Jewish army, logically (it will not be the one from heaven), which at the end of this defeats the Greeks. The translations, as usual, cause a lot of confusion for those who do not delve into the language before making their interpretations of the texts, and in this case the Hebrew text says that "he grew up to the host of heaven", the Greek speaks *of" to be exalted to the stars of heaven* " or " *great to the power of the heavens* ", while the Vulgate reports that he " *was magnified to the strength of heaven* ", that is, that "he grew to heaven". But does this mean? Accepting the use of classical euphemisms that are always evoked in literature, he would be saying that Antiochus exalted himself above the heavenly powers. In chapter 11, starting from verse 30, all this is dealt with in greater detail, but regarding chapter 8 the verse is very curious, since it assumes that Antiochus's actions cause him to "bring down to earth", both *" from among the army* » as « *from among the stars* », so that they are "trodden down".

Although the first two books of the Maccabees address this story, I will attach some relevant quotes to contextualize the theme. Suppose that the trampled army – at first – are the Jewish forces, but when talking about Kokabim (stars, planets, angels) it seems a clear indication of the participation of celestial beings in human affairs. But, how is it that he "tramples" them? If they are glorious beings, of light and dedicated to spiritual work, how do they have to lower themselves to the degree of fighting hand to hand with mortals? The dignity of these angels came to be lowered to the point of leaving their place of holiness to resolve human affairs and rub shoulders with them in personal disputes. For example, Antiochus' high official was about to take the treasure from the temple, but was intervened by angels:

« *But when he was already with his escort next to the Treasury, the Sovereign of spirits and of all Powers manifested himself in such splendor that all those who had dared to come with him, wounded by the power of God, were left without strength and intimidated. . For* **a richly caparisoned horse appeared to them, mounted by a fearsome rider** *, which, throwing itself with impetus, raised its front hooves against Heliodorus. The rider was covered in gold armor. <u>Two other young men of extraordinary vigour, resplendent with their beauty and splendidly dressed, also appeared to him</u> : they stood on either side of him and lashed him without ceasing, beating him to the ground. Heliodorus fell to the ground, wrapped in a dense darkness, and was immediately picked up and carried out on a stretcher. Thus they now carried, unable to fend for himself, the one who had entered the Treasury shortly before, accompanied by a large retinue and all his escort. And all clearly recognized the sovereignty of God. As he lay struck down by divine force, speechless and without hope of salvation, the Jews blessed the Lord, who had glorified his own Place. The Temple, which had been filled with fear and consternation not long before, was now overflowing with joy and jubilation at the manifestation of the Almighty Lord. Immediately, some of Heliodorus's companions begged Onías to invoke the Most High so that he would spare the life of the one who was about to expire. The High Priest, fearing that the king would suspect that the Jews had attacked Heliodorus, offered a sacrifice for his cure. While the High Priest was offering the expiation sacrifice,* **the same young men appeared again to Heliodorus, covered with the same garments and, standing up** *, said to him: "Give thanks* *to the High Priest Onias, because through his intercession the Lord grant life. And now you, who have been punished by Heaven, announce to all the greatness of God's power." Saying this, they disappeared . (2nd Mac. 3:24-34)*

The hand-to-hand friction between angels and humans has been verified throughout history on many occasions - as you can see in my work 'Wandering Stars' (2010) -, but the biblical writings of the Protestant canon already make this very evident, as when « *Yakob was left alone; and a man wrestled with him until daybreak* " (Gen. 32:24), which is assumed to be an angel, or the archangels Gabriel and Michael themselves must have gotten into these conflicts (as Daniel himself addresses later on), even when a prince of Yaheveh's army came to assist Joshua in the capture of Jericho (Joshua 5:13-15), or when an angel massacred 185,000 Egyptian soldiers coming against Judeah in the days of Hezekiah (Isaiah 37:36). . Jewish victory was assured thanks to their trust in the Most High:

« *Timothy, who had already been defeated by the Jews before, after recruiting numerous foreign troops and collecting a considerable number of horses brought from Asia, presented himself with the intention of conquering Judea by arms. As he approached, the Maccabee and his men covered his head with dust and tied their waists with cilices, to plead with God. Prostrated at the foot of the altar, they asked him to show propitiousness to them, making himself an enemy of his enemies and an adversary of his adversaries, as the Law declares. At the end of the plea, they took up their weapons and advanced a good distance outside the city. When they were close to their enemies, they stopped. At dawn, the two sides launched into combat. Some had as a pledge of success and victory, in addition to their courage, their trust in the Lord; the others fought driven only by their courage. At the height of the battle, **the enemies saw five majestic men appear in the sky, mounted on horses with golden bridles, who led the Jews** . These men placed the Maccabee in their midst and, covering him with their weapons, <u>made him invulnerable, while</u>*

they shot arrows and thunderbolts at the adversaries . These, blinded by the brilliance, dispersed in the most complete disorder. Thus twenty thousand five hundred soldiers and six hundred horsemen perished . (2nd Mac. 10:24-31)

« *When the Maccabee gathered his followers, some six thousand in all, he exhorted them not to let themselves be intimidated by the enemies or to be intimidated by the immense crowd of people who came to attack them unjustly. He also encouraged them to fight with enthusiasm, keeping in mind the outrages perpetrated against the Sanctuary, the violence against the humiliated City and the suppression of the customs of their ancestors. "They, he told them, trust in their weapons and in their audacity, but* **we trust in the Almighty God who can undo with a single gesture not only those who attack us, but also the entire world** *."* Then *he listed all the aid with which his ancestors had been favored* , especially in the time of *Sennacherib, when one hundred and eighty-five thousand men died. He reminded them of* **the battle fought in Babylon against the Galatians, when eight thousand Jews went into action along with four thousand Macedonians. On that occasion, the Macedonians found themselves without a way out and the eight thousand Jews,** **_thanks to the help received from Heaven, defeated one hundred and twenty thousand enemies._** *and seized great booty* ." (2nd Mac. 8:16-20)

Not a few were the times in which the angels helped the Jews against the forces of Antiochus:

« *When the supporters of the Maccabee learned that Lysias had besieged the fortress, they began to plead with the Lord with groans and tears, united with the crowd, asking him to send a protective angel to save Israel. Maccabee himself, who was the first to take up arms, exhorted the others to face the danger together with him, in order to save his brothers. They all rushed into battle with great enthusiasm, and while they were still near Jerusalem,* **a horseman dressed in white and brandishing weapons of gold appeared in front of them** *. All unanimously blessed the merciful God, and were inflamed in such a way that they were ready to attack,* *not only against men, but also against the most ferocious beasts and even against iron walls. Thus they advanced in battle order, <u>protected by their heavenly ally</u>, because the Lord had taken pity on them. And rushing like lions against the enemies, they felled eleven thousand soldiers and sixteen hundred horsemen, and all the rest they forced to flee. Most of these escaped wounded and unarmed, and Lysias himself escaped shamefully by fleeing ."* (2nd Mac. 11:6-12)

Daniel tells us that this blasphemous ruler " *has exalted himself to the commander of the army* " (verse 11), but what army is he talking about? And above all, what military commander are you talking about? This is the apparently unclear part of this account, the use of the last word of the quote, "tirmesem", as if he had trampled down the host of heaven, but some interpret it as referring to "outrage" (of the form "Ramas ", where the definition cited there comes from), in terms of also messing directly with these powers that came down. Here it seems to tell us that, even as seen in typical translations, Antiochus exalts himself "against" a military general of an army, but he does not clarify what army he is talking about. However, if we stick to the historical context, the interpretation that seems to fit the most is that not only Antiochus magnifies himself, but also the general of his army. Daniel chapter 11, as I have already said, is more explicit on this, but in this sense Wikipedia tells us of Antiochus:

« On his return, he organized an expedition against Jerusalem, which he sacked. According to the Book of Maccabees, he promulgated several religious ordinances: he tried to suppress the cult of Yahveh, he prohibited Judaism by suspending all kinds of religious manifestations, he ordered that food considered impure be eaten, and he tried to establish the cult of the Greek gods. But the Jewish priest Matatías and his two sons called Maccabees managed to raise the population against him and expelled him. The Jewish holiday of Hanukkah commemorates this fact. » (Wikipedia.org/Antíoco_IV_Epífanes)

Another thing that Daniel anticipates is that because of that "horn" and/or his military chief" *the daily was taken away* " and " *its holy place was taken away* " . The correspondences are obvious, and we can observe that the 'Tamid', or "continual" sacrifice performed by the priests was prohibited by Antiochus, who also " *threw down the foundation of his sanctuary* ". All this desecration is subsequently cited in chapters 11 and 12, and they receive the generic name of 'Shikutz Meshumem' (Abomination that Devastates), of which the image is the one that Daniel also describes at the end of chapter 9, and of which reiterates Jesus Christ in the Eschatological Sermon. Next Daniel adds that an " *army given on the daily in transgression* ", an issue that some interpret as a reference to the fact that the Jewish army was delivered into the hands of Antiochus to be humiliated because of its sin, but this would not be entirely correct historically. What can be seen by reviewing the translation is that Antiochus sends his troops to desecrate the temple, using military force he takes control and promotes sacrilege and abominations, as he quotes later in the extension of this vision, saying that « *with flattery will seduce covenant breakers* ." (Dan. 11:32, R60) I already mentioned it above when quoting First Maccabees 11 to 15:

« *It was then that a group of renegades appeared in Israel who seduced many, saying: "Let us make an alliance with the neighboring nations, because since we separated from them, many evils have befallen us." This proposal was well received, and some of the people went immediately to see the king and he gave them authorization to **follow the customs of the pagans. They built a gymnasium in Jerusalem in the style of the pagans, they hid the mark of circumcision and, reneging on the holy alliance , they joined the pagans and gave themselves up to all kinds of evil* ." (1st Mac. 10-15)

But Daniel, while observing all these things, heard a saint speaking to another saint about the time when this 'Pishá Shmem' (destroying transgression) - which surely refers to the abomination of destruction -:

« Then I heard a saint speak; and another of the saints asked the one who spoke: "How long will the vision of the continuous sacrifice last, the devastating prevarication and the delivery of the sanctuary and the army to be trampled?" And he said: "Until two thousand three hundred evenings and mornings; then the sanctuary will be purified" .» (Dan. 13-14, RVA 95)

« Into the hands of strangers I have delivered it to be plundered, and it will be prey to the wicked of the earth, and they will desecrate it. And I will turn my face away from them, and my secret place will be violated; for invaders will enter it and desecrate it ." (Ezekiel 7:21-22, R60)

Indeed, this abomination did not last, and ended with the purification of the temple. However, we continue to see details that need to be clarified, and although I will qualify when addressing chapter 11 of Daniel, I can anticipate that Antiochus certainly took the southern country, and "after defeating Egypt, he set out on his way back, in the one hundred and fortieth year. *" and three, and went up against Israel, coming to Jerusalem with a mighty army .*" (1st Mac. 1:20) This is how Daniel was informed of these things that would happen " *many days* " (Dan. 8:26) after him, and it was so hard for him to hear all this that he was broken and even sick for a long time. several days. The prophet knew that these things had to happen as references to the time of the end, but it does not mean that it was "the end of ends", but rather one of the scenarios that set a series of guidelines that must occur for this Aeon (it was) conclude. The vision about Antiochus included in its context some such "2,300 evenings and mornings", from the beginning of the desecration of the temple until its purification. The use of the definition of "evening and morning" instead of "day" could be interpreted as an allusion to a time of darkness. In other words, a period of spiritual warfare. The saint ends by explaining to Daniel here:

" *And at the end of their reign, when the transgressors come to the full, a king of haughty countenance and understanding riddles will arise. And his power will be strengthened, but not with his own strength; and it will cause great ruins, and it will prosper, and it will do arbitrarily, and it will destroy the strong and the people of the saints. With his sagacity he will make deceit prosper in his hand; and in his heart he will magnify himself, and without warning he will destroy many; and he will rise up against the Prince of princes, but he will be broken, though not by the hand of man."* (Dan. 8:23-25, R60)

Those 4 whose reign had ended before Antiochus' time were Ptolemy, Lysimachus, Cassander, and Seleucus (his own direct ancestor, basically as after great-great-grandfather). This Antiochus is the one who seems to be evoked here and who defeats the saints, that is, the Hebrew people. It is not entirely clear who is the 'sar sarim' (chief of chiefs) to whom he refers. Logically it cannot be Yeshua (Jesus), since they were at least 160 years away from his birth; nor could it be some priest, as this was established just after the purification of the Temple when the Hasmonean priesthood was established. Furthermore, in the Hebrew priest is not 'sar', but 'Kohen'. Now, could it be the Romans? Or the Persians? The Persian ruler was called by the Persians and peoples subject to the empire "king of kings", but the Hebrews were not going to call him "melej ha.melejim" (king of kings), since that is a title for the Messiah and even for God. The text reads 'sar sarim' (chief of chiefs), which the sages translated into the Septuagint as 'Apoléias Andron' (destroying man). Said explanation does not clarify the matter, but what can clarify it is the context of the facts and the Hebrew jargon, since the Jews were organized by assemblies and named 'sarim' (principal), and among them, the most reputable was the ' prince of the people', that is, the principal of all the chiefs.

By writing "not by human hand" (vers. 25), they significantly modified the story, because it does not say anything like that: "*yad ishber*" (his hand will be broken), where hand is a Hebrew euphemism for "power", like it also reads in the Septuagint: "jeirí syntrípsei" (shattered hand). Now, the archangel Gabriel had already spoken of these rulers when he said that the 'sar' (chief) of the Persian kingdom opposed him (he stood "in front", lit.) for 3 weeks so that he had not been able to reach before Daniel (ch. 10:13). This assumption could be correct in light of what the chronology encompasses:

« *Antiochus, in campaign against the Parthian Empire, reaped some successes, conquering Elam and Babylon. While organizing a punitive expedition to retake Israel personally, he died of tuberculosis* . (Wikipedia) We can see that Daniel and the other sources match perfectly, every time the Romans threaten him (chap. 11:44), he goes against Jerusalem, but at the time of rebelling the Maccabees begin to lose power in the area; He goes against the Persians and gains ground, but when he wants to return against the Jews, death, but not in war or by anyone's hand. The phrase of Daniel 8:25 was translated as "not by human hand", but that has nothing to do, neither with the Latin translation, nor with the Greek, nor with the original Aramaic version. It only says that his strength (which in Aramaic and Hebrew is said "iad" (hand) as a representation of power) would be destroyed. Nor does it affirm anything that he will be "broken", only that his plan to defeat this "man" is "stopped", and "his hand ceases and is broken", that is, his power is reduced, finished.

We can conclude that this vision is about the struggle between Persia and Greece (events that took place in the 5th century BC), because although much of it is also a problem with the Jews, it concludes with an attempt to subdue the already weakened Persians. , which is the time of Antiochus's death. We begin by seeing that Alexander stood up to the Persians and from the battle of Gaugamela the Hellenes took over the Persians and Alexander began his victory over Darius III and his empire. Here this vision ended, that is, this war began to end, and shortly after Alexander died in his own bed, not in the war or by anyone's intervention (there are several theories about how he died, but none have been proven and all three are known they differ from each other, although they agree that he did not die in the war but in his "mansion", the palace that had been Nebuchadnezzar's), but something similar happened to Antiochus. Antiochus in his time had desecrated the temple of Jerusalem, and that is a well-known topic in Jewish history, where they even say that the devastating abomination was that, in the year 168 BC. C., and refuse to accept as such that of the years 66 to 135 d. C., since they know that the context, if accepted, would make it clear that the Messiah really appeared in the first century AD. C., even so, his interpretation is not completely wrong.

V. VISION OF THE SEVENTY "WEEKS"

One of the theological debate chapters par excellence, regarding the prophet Daniel, is 9; basically the end of it. It was the first year of King Ahasuerus – possibly Xerxes I – when Daniel prayed for his people for the sin they committed and for which the evil that Jeremiah had prophesied came upon them. Praying for his atonement and for the mercy of Yahweh to come upon them to be restored, the archangel Gabriel came and let him know that the intercession of the prophet had been heard and the guidelines that would take place to redeem his people had been determined:

« *I was still speaking and praying, and confessing my sin and the sin of my people Israel, and poured out my prayer before Yaheveh Elohei (my God) for the holy mountain of my God; I was still speaking in prayer, when the man Gabriel, whom I had seen in the vision at the beginning, flying swiftly, came to me about the time of the evening sacrifice. And he made me understand, and spoke to me, saying: Daniel, now I have come out to give you wisdom and understanding. At the beginning of your prayers the order was given, and I have come to teach it to you, because you are very loved. Therefore understand the command, and understand the vision .*" (Dan. 9:20-23, R60)

The point where the great entanglements come is in the following verses, especially for a matter of Hebrew and Aramaic languages, and puns from said languages. Since writing verbatim what Daniel says in the following verses is almost like returning to the same erroneous base from which interpreters and theologians start, it is important to clarify that the use of Hebrew transliteration is more necessary here than in other references. The verse begins by writing that « *Shiim Shbiim leave the amech* », although we can also write these first words as "shabuim shibim", as emphasized by the Masoretes, or simply "shabeim shabeim".

The Aramaic term Shibím Shibím, which translates as 70 weeks, but what does that definition mean? We have in Hebrew letters the Shin, the Beit, the Ain, the Yod and the Mem, but since these last two denote a plural in the phrase – masculine, by the way – we will focus for the moment on the first three. The letters Shin and Beit are cognate of the form 'Sheb' (to sit, usually read as 'Isheb' or 'Shebah'), which in Aramaic means 'old', and in Hebrew it forms 'Sib' (hoary, old); it is also a root of 'Shub' (to return, to return, to repent). As for 'Shebah', which is assumed to be relative to 'sit', it also translates 'to take' or 'to lead captive', although all these words do not seem to necessarily have anything to do with the context of what we are legend about. here.

When we add the Ain to the letters Shin and Beit, they change the idea to identify the idea of quenching, satisfying, abundance; swear; or seven. What would be the plural of these? Satisfactions? Abundances? oaths? "Sevens"? But there is another component, and that is that there may be extra letters or conjugations that give another value to the word, such as 'Shbua', which is the same definition but with a 'Vav' before the Ain, and which means 'week'. This conformation of letters is accepted as the one to which Daniel would refer, but even so, that does not explain how it appears twice, since it would be translated as "weeks weeks". Ergo, we read "weeks", but the truth is that it is a contradictory way of referring to this, since, for example, the 'Feast of Weeks' is called 'Chag Shabuot', not 'Chag Shabeim'. The ending 'ot' is for feminine plurals, and is applicable to "week". However, in Leviticus 12:5 we read that it says 'Shbaim' (the Masoretes wrote 'Shbuaim'), which they translate as 'two weeks', since in Hebrew and Aramaic, a plural, although it is not accompanied by a specific unit of quantity, is understood as two quantities or units.

In other cases, instead of saying "Shabuot" they say "Shabatot" (Shin, Beit and Tau). Because? Because Saturday is the seventh day, it is called 'seventh' (shabat). The same with respect to the week, which is called "shabua", from "Sheba" (seven), that is, it would be something like "septenio" (in Greek 'hebdómada', which means "set of seven"). If we look at the Vulgate, it tells us "septuagint ebdomades" (seventy seven). And if he is talking about seventy sets of seven? Within numerology it is possible to understand in a high probability that this could be – among other things – a computation of "70 x 7", that is, 490, which could be the time elapsed from the return of the deportation to Babylon until the Messiah. In 538 B.C. C. the Jews can return, and in 515 the reconstruction of the temple is completed (which adds 70 years since in 586 BC Nebuchadnezzar had taken them captive, as Jeremiah warned), so 490 would have ended on the 48 a. C., which is the period of completion of the Hasmonean priesthood and the beginning of the Herodian reign. If, on the contrary, the calculation from the reconstruction of the temple (515 BC) is accepted, the 490 years would effectively be completed at the time of the birth of Jesus Christ, around the year 25 BC. c.

If it is taken into account that Herod died in the year 4 a. C., and in those days Joseph the carpenter lived with his wife and Yeshua (Jesus) in Egypt, it must be added that they already lived in Bethlehem years before, when they had to flee due to the massacre of the children. According to the Ev. Ammonius, that time in Egypt was 7 years, and if Herod was informed by the astronomers of the date of the sign about the Messiah that made him look for children under 2 years of age, we can consider that Yeshua must have been born around the year 12 BC. C., which is very close to the calculation of 490 years. Not only that, it is also quite close to the date that Herod himself began the improvements to the temple (19 BC). But then, 7-70 was 490 years? if the computation is correct, it could be closely related, but it is not the only point to consider. If we read 'Shbua' as week, and 'Shbaim' as weeks, what is the plural of 'Shbuah' (oath)? Ezekiel 21:23 uses the words "Shbuei Shbuot", seven weeks? It seems not. The interpretation and context that encompasses the dialogue speaks of 'solemn oaths', which strangely the Vulgate translated as 'sabbatorum otium' (being 'otium' the root of the English 'oath' (oath), but 'sabbatorum' alluding to Shabbat). Also Habakkuk 3:9 writes 'Shabuot' in the sense of oaths or curses.

The reference to "week" is interpreted by some to be relative to "seven" years, given the relationships of these terms to 7, and that could be related to the calculation made by some, which I mentioned a moment ago. Despite this, I have to clarify that this relationship has been assumed by a passage from Genesis 29:18, where it says " *abadeja shba shanim* " , that is, " *I will work for you seven years* " , where the word 'Shba' not only means "seven" but is the root of "week" (ie SEVEN [days]), and therefore, before meaning "week", means simply "7". Apart from this, it means "oath" or "conjuration", which is why in Hebrew idioms and culture, the number 7 was used as something sacred, an oath, something pragmatic or sealed, something related to a curse, something determining or great. Hence, in verse 27 it says « *malé shbua* » (sufficient oath), to refer to the fact of completing the agreed "7", although they have translated "the week of this".

Consequently, if the text of Daniel spoke of 70 weeks, it would literally include these events in about one year and four months (490 days). Due to everything that Daniel refers to next, that does not make much sense. If we assume they were "curses", that doesn't make much sense either. If he spoke to us about oaths, how should we understand him? As I said, in Hebrew we have the masculine plural "im" at the end of a word, and the feminine plural "ot" at the end of a word. Firstly Shbim, Shabim or Shabuim are conjurations, oaths or seventy, while Shiot, Shabiot or Shabuot are weeks. To the naked eye, without nekudot (dots added by the Masoretes), the two words would read the same. The relationship of the root is the same "7", both in Hebrew and in Aramaic, and from there comes the idea of the concept of 7 as a cycle or great complex of something, since it combines the idea of a weekly cycle (7 periods of light) with an oath. Shbim shabim could be more accurately "70 conjurations", which in a symbolic sense can be understood as 70 patterns related to computations and cycles (hence its relationship with the word "shabua", that is, week, and with the possible 490 years since Cyrus I, or since the reconstruction of the Temple).

What's more, if the computation of time were calculated under the prism of 70-70, it would give us 4,900 compared to what this is for those who understand numerology and astronomical cycles, and that it could be 4,900 days (almost 13 and a half years). , or 4,900 weeks (700 years). This last arithmetic gibberish could also be the time elapsed from the order of Cyrus (538 BC) until the expulsion of the Jews from their land (AD 135), although some years would be left over, since the 700 would be fulfilled. about AD 162 C. but leaving aside so many numbers, let's analyze what it was that had to be carried out or fulfilled. According to the translation of Reina Valera, from 1960, it would say:

" *Seventy weeks are determined upon your people and upon your holy city, to finish the transgression, and put an end to sin, and atone for iniquity, to bring lasting justice, and seal vision and prophecy, and anoint the Holy of saints .*» (Dan. 9:24)

The original text tells us about 6 things: 1°. Jala hapesha (catch transgression), 2nd. Lechatem [lehatem] hataot [hatat] (seal the sin), 3rd. Lekaper on (cover guilt), 4th. Lehabia tzedek olamim (bring justice-righteousness of the aeons), 5th. Lechatem chazon venebiá (sealing vision and prophecy), 6°. Lemashej kodesh kodashim (to anoint the holy of holies). Regarding the first point, we know that Yeshua took over the transgression (since "jala" is to imprison), as Isaiah had prophesied, affirming that «having loaded *the transgressions of all of us* . » (ch. 53:6) Who are "all of us"? Isaiah was a Jew, and he spoke of his people, as Daniel was told: " *about your people ...* " . How does Yeshua catch transgression? He offers himself as a sacrifice, and we Christians remember this as the "sacrifice of the lamb", an analogy to the blood of the Passover lamb in Egypt, which Jesus Christ himself celebrated the night he was handed over, when blessing the wine he said, « *Drink from it all; for this is my blood of the new covenant, which is shed for many for the remission of sins.* » (Matt. 26:27-28, R60) . And why did he say this? Because he fulfilled what Daniel said in the following verse, which, as you will see, announces a new Covenant, the one that Jeremiah also warned about:

« *Behold, the days are coming, says Yahweh, in which I will make a new covenant with the house of Israel and with the house of Judah. Not like the covenant I made with their fathers on the day I took their hand to lead them out of the land of Egypt; because they invalidated my pact, although I was a husband for them, says Yaheveh. But this is the pact that I will make with the house of Israel after those days, says Yaheveh: I will put my law in his mind, and I will write it in his heart; and I will be their God, and they will be my people. And no one will teach his neighbor anymore, nor any one his brother, saying: Know Yaheveh; because everyone will know me, from the smallest of them to the greatest, says Yaheveh; for I will forgive their wickedness, and I will remember their sin no more .*" (Jer. 31:31-34, R60)

The covenant that Daniel spoke of is the "new covenant." The Aramaic text does not say "confirmed" but rather Gabir, which means "strong", referring to the fact that there will be a powerful pact, supporting other prophecies of a new pact, better than the previous one. That covenant begins with Yeshua and the blood of that new covenant. Regarding the second point mentioned, that of "sealing sin", it could be interpreted that it has to do with the death of Christ, according to the law of Moses, and then the above? The one refers to the violation of the law of Moses that is invalidated by the New Covenant, and the other refers to controlling and putting an end to the power of the forces of destiny that carry out the "effects" to the "causes" that we call sin. Then in the third point he talks about "covering the fault", which is the fact of protecting the faults made by the person, in what sense?

In that the "curriculum" - so to speak - of the person is not stained by his wrong actions, and the individual is covered and protected, defended and justified. The kerubim on the Ark of the Covenant covered the entire receptacle with their wings, which possessed the symbols of power (Aaron's rod), the law (the two tables) and the truth (manna). The Hebrew concept of "lecaper" implies taking care of something, protecting it and keeping it. The Messiah is the one who presides over whether or not to redeem sins, and he is the lawyer for his servants when they make mistakes, because he defends them by justifying them. That is why Yeshua went to live in Capernaum before beginning his ministry, since 'Kaper-Nachum' means "to cover [making] comfort", or "to cover by consoling". These three points of the 6 that were to be fulfilled among those 62 (of the 70) are clearly strictly and decidedly related to the last hours of Christ before everything was consummated (when he said, "it is finished ") .

Regarding the 4th point, we also know that the Messiah brought the truth of the kingdom of heaven, the teachings on justice and rectitude, and the legitimization of the law (he did not come to abrogate but to fulfill). Then we have the 5th, which is the context where all the vision and prophecy are sealed, in an elementary sense the fulfillment of the prophecies about the coming of the Anointed One, but in a deeper sense it is "sealing" the "prophecies" and " visions" about Yaheveh's plan for humanity. That is, Daniel was told that this was the theme of the end, telling him "this is sealed until the time of the end", plus said seals were released by the Lamb and announced to his servant John, so that the end and justice may come. and eternal peace. In addition to this, Yeshua's mission was not only to teach "eternal justice" and to give his life as a ransom for many and to cover their faults, but to complete the entire project - excuse the redundancy - which influences completing the decisive things that were to come. with the Messiah to end this era. Finally, the 6th point tells us about the anointing of the most holy place that was performed every time the temple was rebuilt, but as we know, the Third Temple made by men is not the true temple, but the one that comes from heaven: the New Jerusalem. It is not entirely clear if the elementary interpretation of this is correct, as it could be a number of things: First, we could assume that it refers to the cleansing of the temple, but that had nothing to do with Yeshua and predates him . ; second, it could refer to Yeshua as a symbol of the sanctum sanctorum, but it would only be an interpretation; third, to anoint the New Jerusalem, but there is no proof whatsoever to support this theory; fourth, to anoint a representative of God, which would be most holy, but what is the point of this and what does it have to do with the question? Despite this, we could consider that the second option could be correct, not so much for representing Yeshua the holy sanctorum, but for being able to receive the title of "holy of holies", or for what could be read from Hebrew as "the Messiah". saint of saints".

We have that the 70 conspiracies are organized in three groups (7 and 62, and 1), starting at 7+62 from the order to restore and rebuild Jerusalem (around the year 539 BC) until the Mashij nagid (anointed prince, that is, the Messiah), which was in the year 11-13 BC, approx., until 25-27 AD. C., approx. It could be correct to consider that the first 7 were from the order of Cyrus I until the reconstruction of the temple, assuming that the Maccabean and Hasmonean stages fall within that period in which these events must take place until the 62nd birthday of the Messiah. Here we already have the fulfillment of the 69, and only 1 would be missing. It is notorious that by dividing them into 7 and 62, he is assuming that they deal with two different groups of things, the return of the Jews from Babylon and the rebuilding of the wall of Jerusalem and the temple are the first 7 shibim, and then the mission of the Messiah, the other 62 shibim, being things planned by the deity, although they had different contexts. These were determined on two things: 1. his people (the Jews) and his holy city (Jerusalem), since when saying "your", they refer to Daniel, and the Hebrew word Amej is "your people", Daniel being a Jew . Daniel belonged to the nobles who were taken to be part of Nebuchadnezzar's advisers and in essence these facts were primarily relative to the Jewish people: with them the law of

Sinai (the old covenant) began, and as Jeremiah said, with them would come a new covenant (a new covenant).

« *Know, then, and understand, that from the issuance of the order to restore and build Jerusalem until the Messiah the Prince, there will be seven weeks, and sixty-two weeks; the plaza and the wall will be rebuilt in distressing times. And after sixty-two weeks the Messiah will be killed, but not for himself; and the people of a prince who is to come will destroy the city and the sanctuary; and its end will be with a flood, and until the end of the war the devastation will last.* » (Dan. 9:25-26, R60)

We observe in this verse 25 the confirmation of what was said previously, and the emphasis at the end of the sentence, " *in troublesome times* ", since it encompasses the conflicts between Persians and Greeks, conflicts that at certain times also affected the Jews. But, what happens after this Maccabean-Hasmonean period, when the Persians were no longer there, nor were the Greeks a problem? The period of the Messiah arrives, which is under the occupation of the emerging new empire: Rome. The text does not say that the Messiah appears and is later assassinated, but directly says that he is "murdered", but how does he come to be assassinated and where? At what point does he first appear on the scene only to be killed? This reinforces the previous explanation that the Messiah is related to the 62 shabeim, that these begin with his appearance and end with his assassination. They make it clear to Daniel that this death "is not for its own sake", that is, it is not like that because yes, there is a reason for being, something behind it, a purpose, and it revolves - as we Christians already know - in accordance with the work of the own messiah. Even so, the Hebrew passage actually says, " *ve ein lo* ," which RVA 95 translates " *and nothing will remain for him* ," while the Greek writes " *and will not be* " or " *and will not be judged* ." Basically « *ve ein lo* » is "and does not have", which can be understood as "and will not be" or "and they will not have it".

Thus, in that period of time " *the square and the wall will be built again* ", he adds, " *in distressing times* ", which was in the middle of the war between the Persian dynasties and Alexander's troops, including the distribution of power between their kings (his power passed to his 4 generals (Dan. 11:4)) during the struggle of the Maccabean brothers and the subsequent Hasmonean assembly until the reign of Herod. Then the story continues: " *And after sixty-two weeks the Messiah will be killed, but not for himself...* " He speaks of the assassination of the Messiah, and then " *and the people of a prince who is to come will destroy the city and the sanctuary; and its end will be with a flood, and until the end of the war the devastation will last* ." A prince? Yes. The invasion of Judeah was during a change of power in Rome (the supposed suicide of Nero) and the conspiracy after the death of Galba and Otho. The Emperor Vespasian was proclaimed king, and consequently his son Titus (prince) was sent by his father to end the escalation that had begun against Judeah (where Jerusalem had been besieged). The flood was the Roman legions, and the devastation was the death of more than a million Jews and proselytes who had gone up to that Pesach (Passover), involved in the three wars that destroyed the identity and nation of the Jewish people for almost 1800 years. (until the Balfour declaration).

During all this period of time, from the 62 conspiracies that the Messiah fulfills, " *he will confirm the pact with many* ". That covenant is the New Alliance that was established by many for the forgiveness of sins. And at the end of that period of the birth and impulse of Christianity, the disaster occurred: " *he will make the sacrifice and the offering cease* ." After the defeat of the Jewish troops to the north, Judeah was taken and Jerusalem besieged, but a landmark in the history of the Jews and of Israel to this day was the end of the priestly liturgy. The siege of Jerusalem and the war forced the cessation of ritual sacrifices and offerings in the temple, which were never performed again (because the Roman soldiers found a fissure in the wall and burst, entered the city and massacred all , they set fire to the temple and it collapsed). When one reads the Vulgate it is even more explicit, literally saying, " *[the end of] the wafers and the sacrifices* ."

The next part is what happened some 30 years later. He adds, then, that " *a prince who is to come will destroy the city and the sanctuary* ", speaking of the events that have occurred since the year 66, when the prince (Titus) destroyed Jerusalem and the temple. Then he also predicts the end of these abominable episodes such as a flood - of Roman legions -, and until the end of the Shmemot (desolations) in the second Judeo-Roman war (115-117 AD) and the third Judeo-Roman war. Roman (132-135 AD). The taking of Judeah was almost the end of the quelling of the Jewish rebellion against the Roman Empire in the first open and official war between the Jews and the empire. The campaign was directed by Vespasian, in charge of ending the rebels, but when his troops arrived to besiege Jerusalem, Nero died, supposedly by suicide. Vitellus defeats Otho, who had assassinated Galba, Nero's successor, and Vespasian sent his troops to Italy while he secured grain supplies in Egypt. During this time of chaos in Rome, Vitellius falls and the Senate subsequently proclaims Vespasian as emperor. When Vespasian gave up his takeover of Jerusalem, he put his eldest son, Titus, in command of the troops and the mission of victory over Judeah.

This quote that tells us about the "end" with flooding is not literal, but a metaphor. The "end" with inundation is a euphemism for "washing away". Consider the facts, 3 Roman legions (each of almost 5,000 men), are 15,000 infantry soldiers: XII Fulminata had 5,120 infantry and 120 cavalry, V Macedonica had between 5,000 and 6,000 men, and XV Apollinaris had 3,500 more men. auxiliaries. After razing the Jewish revolt in the north and later in Judeah, these units arrived in Jerusalem razing and crushing all opposition. That was the 'Shtef' (flood, destroy) of which the text speaks. The verse does not speak of 'Mabul' (deluge), as some have tried to suggest, but of 'Shtef' (flood, wash away, wash away). Scholars say that in Daniel 9:26 the idea alludes to something impetuous, although RVA understands it as "cataclysm." An example with the same word in Proverbs 27:4, in the composition, « *shétef af* » , translates "barrage of fury", a euphemism for "impetuous fury"; In other words, destroy something impetuously. Then he says that " *until the end of the war the devastation will last* ", since he is clarifying that this "flood" is a military invasion, a context of warfare, and that all the misfortunes that were to befall the Jews would continue until the end of the war. definitively concluded the war at all, which took place in the year 135 d. C., when the Jews were expelled from their land.

« *Cumano ordered all the troops, taking up arms, to concentrate on the Antonia fortress which, as we said, dominates the Temple. The crowd, at the sight of the soldiers, terrified, hastened to flee; As the exits were narrow and they believed that the enemies were chasing them, many of them perished in these narrow places. There were 25,000 deaths in that tumult; so that the festivity became a date of mourning, in such a way that everyone, forgetful of the sacrifices and prayers, began to lament and moan .* » (Antiquities of the Jews 5:3, Flavio Josefo) Until those days the "continual sacrifices" to Nero also ceased by order of Eleazar ben Hanania, in charge of the care of the Temple, coinciding, all this, with Daniel. From this point no more sacrifices were celebrated, since this revolt, although it was the first of three decisive wars between Jews and Romans, was the one that resulted in the burning and subsequent destruction of the temple (without a temple there are no sacrifices, because there was the altar of offerings and holocausts) about 3 and a half years later (in 70 AD).

« *And for another week he will confirm the pact with many; in the middle of the week he will make sacrifice and oblation cease. Later with the multitude of abominations will come the desolator, until the consummation comes, and what is determined is poured out on the desolator.* » (Dan. 9:27, R60)

This last verse concludes this topic, but as in the previous cases, the translation is not entirely reliable. There are versions that say that the one who would take the city and end everything would be the one who would "confirm" this pact and make the sacrifice and offering cease, nothing to do with the Hebrew version. We can read that it says " *vehagabor brit lerabim shbua achad* " (and a greater pact [there will be] for many [in] a conspiracy), that is, it begins a new pact with many (including the Gentiles). Then, halfway through this cycle of "7" is when the sacrifices stop, that is, temple services (year 66 AD), because from that same Easter, of that year, never again, until the day Today, animal sacrifices were not performed nor were all the other Levitical rituals performed, nor was there any more temple. Because? Because it had to be fulfilled, since no more sacrifices made sense, since Christ was the true and last sacrifice. The termination of the temple's existence was the next point of this New Covenant, because now many were to apply the concept of "temple" to their own body. The first half of the last Shbua is the work of Christ and his apostles up to the siege of Jerusalem.

The beginning of the last week was the period of Christianity since the ascension of Christ and it went through this time of destruction of Judeah. The end of that week ends there, where the following sequence of events enters, which is what John predicts, but it must be fulfilled with the destruction of the "desolate" that devastated Judeah, that is, Rome (the Vatican empire, etc.) . So what it means is that in that period he would affirm-strengthen (not "confirm", as they translated) a "New Pact" (started with the Last Supper (years 27-33 AD), and the Christian movement that began and was consolidated by the apostolic work and the manifestation of the Holy Spirit), established for many. That New Pact enters within that last Shbua of the 70, and its end is the other "jetzi" (half), where the sacrifices and offerings cease (66-70 AD), and the desolator (Rome) it comes with all the multitude of abominations (which includes the idea of desecration, from people, to the holy city and temple with all its sacred things), an issue that continued for two more wars until ending the Jewish opposition and expelling our people of Judah.

The pact is not confirmed. In Hebrew 'confirm' is Leasher, and there it does not say Leasher but Ha.Gabir (strengthen, affirm, strengthen, the strong, make strong). The covenant is "established" and "affirmed" during the first century AD. C. with the Christian movement that becomes "strong". The New Covenant that was born and strengthened by the work of Christianity is what he is talking about. The continuous sacrifice made on the Altar ceased hours before the siege of Jerusalem, at Easter in the year 66 AD. C. Ve.ha.gabir = "ve" is what for us is the copulative conjunction "and"... example: "he and you", the cat and the dog", "up and down" // "ha" is the article that for us is "la", "el", "los", "las" // "Gabir" is the conjugation of 'Giboa' (strong, great), in the form "strengthen" // "Brit" is pact or alliance // "la" is about or towards // "rabim" is many or great // "shabua" in this almost yes it is "week", while in the other cases appears "Shabim" and "shabim" (seventy, oaths) // "ajad" is one or unique. So here it only says "and the strengthening of the covenant over many week one". Since it is literal, you have to understand the syntax, which a translator doesn't give you and a non-Hebrew translator doesn't necessarily know: "and a covenant grows-strengthen for many in a week."

But what happened in the other half of the "week"? « *Afterward, with the multitude of abominations, the desolator will come, until the consummation comes, and what is determined is poured out on the desolator* . » (Dan. 9:27, RVA 60) So it was, once the sacrifices in the temple were suspended, desolation came: all Judea under fire, millions of Jewish dead, destruction of the great wall, destruction of Jerusalem, destruction of the temple and final expulsion of the Jews. The end of Judea was "like" a flood, because the Jews had never faced so many armies. Rome was virtually invincible, and the Jews, having already defeated Galatian, Hellenic, and Egyptian forces, believed their early victories against the Romans to the north would end well. Once Rome defeats Judea, "above" is determined what will be its end.

The Hebrew passage does not say "later, with the crowd." Write « *ve.al knaf* » (and on the wing), which is a Hebrew designation used to refer to the Temple of Jerusalem. The text says « *ve.al knaf shikutzim meshomem* », which means, "and on the wing there will be abominations of desolation". Already before the incident, Archelaus had killed many of those who were working in the Easter preparation services, although some managed to flee to the mountains. After this, as Daniel had said, the city was taken, since the cessation of services occurred several times until they finally stopped after the extension of the siege of the city. The prophecy indicates that the most holy place would be desecrated, and not only that, but devastated with all kinds of abominable, detestable or "diabolical" things. The last Shbei began with the Passover of the lamb and ended with the destruction of Judeah, and that destruction, as Flavio Josephus describes in 'The Jewish Wars' was unimaginable, with a death toll of nearly 1 million Jews and proselytes that had risen to that easter He defines this objectively as a "wasting":

« *Tito, as a man who knew the twists and turns of war, silently concealed the importunate voices of the soldiers; Later, when the city was taken by force of arms, he often required me to take whatever I wanted from the sack of my land, which he gave me permission to do; but I, since **my land was devastated** , I had no other greater consolation in my misfortunes than to ask for free people, which, together with the sacred books, the emperor granted me of good will .*»

« ... **all Judea would be, without anyone remaining, destroyed and devastated** ...»

« *I will not be able to particularly count the wickedness of all these, and to say how much I would like the least I can, **I do not think that there was a city at any time in the whole world that suffered such** , nor do I believe that there was a nation in the world so ferocious and so enough for* *all wickedness and knavery: they also cursed, finally, the Jews themselves, for appearing less impious and less bad against foreigners; but they still confessed what they were, that is, serfs, slaves and bastard people, without honor and without nobility; not natural Jews, but a bad and very perverse generation. Finally, they themselves* **destroyed the city** *, and they were the cause of <u>this sad victory for the Romans, and they themselves devastated the city</u> , and* **brought fire to the temple** *, so that it would not come so quickly, almost with their own hands. Having therefore seen the upper part of the city burn, they did not grieve, nor did they weep for them, finding themselves among the Romans who mourned for it and* <u>**regretted such destruction**</u> ..." (The Wars of the Jews. Titus Josephus Flavius, AD 90)

« *According to Flavio Josefo, the immediate causes of the revolt, in 66, were a pagan sacrifice before the entrance of the synagogue of Caesarea Maritima, followed by the diversion of 17 talents from the treasury of the Temple of Jerusalem, by the procurator Gessius Florus. The decisive act that meant the break with Rome was the decision of Eleazar ben Hanania, in charge of the care of the Temple, to no longer accept the daily sacrifice for the emperor* . » (Wikipedia)

Here the continuous sacrifice ceases and the temple is desecrated (abomination), with that legionary "desolation". The Septuagint is even more explicit in the context, saying that the attack came on the " *holy [place]* ", that is, the temple, and the Vulgate reiterates it, which directly says " *in the temple* ". As I said, the original version, the Hebrew, says " *on the wing* ", which in the Hebrew culture symbolically referred to the most holy place (the sancta sanctorum), where the "wing" (symbol of protection) of God was represented in the wings of the kerubim that covered the mercy seat where Aaron's rod, the decalogue, and a portion of manna were kept (that is, the most sacred thing that the world had and that had been given by God to Israel as a symbol of the alliance with this town). The original text only says that " *detestable abominations* " would fall on the wing , and the concept refers to the idea that the Hebrews had through Moses to desecrate something sacred. This had already happened in the year 168 a. C., when Antiochus IV Epiphanes "defiled" the temple (1 Mac. 1:54, 6:7), and that is what the rabbis teach was the abomination of desolation predicted by Daniel, but said event was not the only one that it falls within the description of an "abomination" of "desolation."

The Abomination of Desolation is a situation. The ravager is an entity. Various uses of "abomination" and "desolation" appear in Daniel, namely, 'Shikutz Mishmem' (Abomination Destroying, Abomination of Desolation), 'Shikutzim' (Abominations, Detestable), 'Shikutz Meshomem' (Abomination Desolation), ' Shmem' (Destroying, Desolating), 'Shikutzim Meshomem' (Destroying Abominations). Regarding the 'Shmem' (devastater), since it is Rome who "devastates" the region and fulfills all this, she is the Devastater. The text announces a New Covenant that initiates and strengthens the Messiah, the destruction of the Second Temple after the coming of the Messiah, and warns that whoever carries out all this sacrilege will receive what is determined at the end. The purpose of the 70 conspiracies was to restore the Holy Place (the first 7), cover iniquity and eliminate sin, as well as seal the vision and prophecy (the 62 that the Messiah developed), and start the New Covenant, while in At the same time the destruction of Jerusalem (the Shabua) was unleashed, which is the key parameter to define the beginning of the end of time as prophesied.

The text tells us « *iashbit, zebej ve.minjah* », that is, « *cease, sacrifices and tributes* ». Since the text has a dividing line in the original, I could assume it meant that the New Covenant is strengthened and there ends the first half of a Shbua (the last program of 7 guidelines), and then the sacrifices and gifts or offerings. to the altar, as well as the holy place itself, would be overwhelmed with detestable and abominable things. In either case, the site slows down the priestly and liturgical services that were held until then, and we could have gone deeper into this if it weren't for the unfortunate fact that Daniel's Qumran scrolls only account for 48% of its content. , and precisely these last verses of chapter 9 are not preserved – and this would have given us the possibility of looking for some translation of the fragments to make a comparative analysis -.

« The arrows and darts that they shot, with the force of the machines and devices they had, reached the temple and the altar, and hit those who were there celebrating their sacrifices; and many who had come from the last parts of the world with great diligence to see the most holy place, were killed standing before the altar and the sacrifices: and they filled it with their blood, as it should be highly adored by all the Greeks and barbarians . »

« It happened, then, in the end, that everything that was around the temple was burned, and the city was made a square or field to fight the same natives and citizens of it; and almost all the wheat was burned, which could have sufficed for many years for the fenced in: they were finally defeated and imprisoned by hunger, which they would not have been, if they themselves had not caused it and had searched for it. The town was divided into parts, no less than if it were a large body, the city being fought, partly by the scoundrels and traitors that were among them, and partly by the neighbors and people who lived nearby. » (The Wars of the Jews, Tito Flavio Josefo)

Although Josephus was no longer alive by the time the Second and Third Wars between the Jews and the Romans took place, the disastrous end of the Hebrew people in their land is known from other sources. The temple was destroyed in the First War, in the year 70, when, and in the spring of the year 71, Tito left for Rome, bequeathing the rest of the sedition to Lucilio Baso, and then to Flavio Silva. Without an altar there were no more sacrifices, without a temple there were no more offerings, and so it is until today that there is still no temple in Jerusalem. This was the punishment that fell on the Jews, and that abomination did not end in that war, but the Desolator (Rome) ended all resistance for almost 70 more years, that is, "until the consummation comes " , when everything had to be completed, fulfilled.

« *In the summer of the year 70 the Romans, having broken the walls of Jerusalem, entered and sacked the city. They first attacked the Antonia Fortress and then occupied the temple, which <u>was burned and destroyed</u> on the 9th day of the Jewish month of Av of the same year; the following month Herod's citadel fell .*

« *After the revolt,* **all of Judea became a province in ruins** *, with <u>Jerusalem reduced to rubble and the Temple destroyed</u> . According to Jewish-Roman author Flavius Josephus, approximately 1,100,000 Jews died and 97,000 were captured and enslaved; current estimates put the death toll at between 600,000 and 1,300,000 Jews. From a historical point of view, the defeat of the Jews was one of the causes of the Diaspora —numerous Jews dispersed after losing their State and some of them were sold as slaves in different parts of the Roman Empire—, and one of the* **biggest catastrophes of Jewish history, which ended the history of the Jewish State in antiquity** *. On the other hand, <u>from the religious point of view, the destruction of the Temple of Jerusalem represented the most important spiritual loss of the Jews</u> , who still today they remember on the day of mourning Tisha b'Av .»* (Wikipedia)

The translation in Spanish in the following point says: " *Then the desolator will come with the multitude of abominations ...*" And it adds, " *until the consummation comes, and what is determined is poured out on the desolator .*" The desolator is Rome, the empire that, as other Hebrew texts describe, is the last empire that must remain until the time of the end. With the fall of Rome (not as a city, but as a structure) " *the times of the Gentiles* " will end (Luke 21:24). So there is something already determined that has to fall on that desolator, but since this punishment has not yet taken place, we must see it as something future: the fall of the great Babylon (the great Harlot). Then, between the years 66 and 70 of the first century AD. C. attempts to help, such as collections from churches at the request of Paul, did not help much (2 Cor. 9:7) and history can tell how the reign of Titus and his successor was, and how Rome Since then it has remained in power, directly or indirectly, passing its hegemony to the Vatican and the Jesuits.

Whatever it looks like, they were ancient events. When one reads Daniel 9, one also sees the same thing, counting from chapter 24 as a summary of the events from the return of the Jews (only 70,000) through the decree of Cyrus (year 537 BC), to the rebuilding of the temple. and his sanctification (519 B.C.) from the days of Zerubbabel to Ezra and Nehemiah. Then chapter 25 emphasizes this process including the first manifestation of the Messiah (Ieshua, in the year 25 AD, approx.) and the reconstruction of the city, the main square, the wall and the beginning of the erection of the foundations. From the temple. Subsequently, chapter 26 mentions the assassination of the Messiah and his estrangement (the fact that he left), and the destruction of Jerusalem by the son of Vespasian (a prince who was to come... because they call him a prince knowing that right in those days of the taking of Judea, the father of Titus, was proclaimed emperor), and of the second temple (70 AD), finally announcing the end of Judeah and exile (135 AD). Verse 27 mentions that the Messiah would confirm his alliance with many from then on (birth of Christianity), and the temple services would stop after the invasion at Easter in AD 66. C. Then he mentions evil using Rome to destroy the people of Judeah and come on "the wing" (a euphemism for the holy of holies in all of Jerusalem). An apocryphal text, apparently somewhat out of tune and forced – or even manipulated – adds some further details:

« *And Titus said: Damn you, Emperor Tiberius, full of ulcers and covered in leprosy, since such a scandal happened during your reign, and since you have made such laws in Judea, in the land of the birth of Our Lord Jesus Christ, where the king and ruler of all the Jews has been seized and put to death, and has not been allowed to come to us, to cure me of leprosy, and deliver me from my disease. And, if those Jews were before me, I would kill them with my own hands, and make them hang on crosses, since they have destroyed my Lord, and my eyes have not been worthy to see his face. And when Titus had spoken thus, the sore on his face disappeared, and he was found perfectly healed. And how many sick were present were healed at the same time. And Titus, with all the people, exclaimed with a loud voice: My God and my king, you, whom I have never seen, and who have healed me, order me to go by sea to the land where you were born, so that take revenge on your enemies, and help, Lord, to destroy them and avenge your death, and deliver them into my hands.* » (Vindica Salvatoris 2:2-4)

« *And, having held council, they left the city of Libya, which is called Burgidalla, and entered the ships, and came to Jerusalem and attacked the kingdom of the Jews, and began to destroy it. And when the kings of the Jews heard the depredations that they were doing, they were terrified and exceedingly disturbed. Then Archelaus was troubled in his speech, and said to his son: My son, receive my kingdom and direct it, and advise yourself with the other kings that exist in the land of Judah, so that you can escape from your enemies. [...] And his son joined the other kings who were under his hierarchy, and they held a council, and they went to Jerusalem with the chiefs of those who were in said council, and they remained there seven years. And Titus and Vespasian agreed to blockade the city, and they did it .*» (Vindica Salvatoris 5:1-5)

VI. VISION OF THE STRUGGLE BETWEEN THE NORTH AND SOUTH KINGDOMS

Daniel 11 tells us about a vision he had, not being asleep, but awake; a vision that consists of another experience with the archangel Gabriel, where this angel informs him about a war of great importance that was to be a follow-up to other events that had already been announced to him. The subject itself does not begin in chapter 11, nor does it end there, but rather it begins earlier, simply being that chapter the one that emphasizes these details, which I have already said that the book of Maccabees deals with. It was the third year of Cyrus' rule (536 BC), possibly over Babylon, and Daniel had a heavenly vision while on the banks of the Jidakel River (which the ancient Persians called 'Tirga', from which it later derived the Greek 'tigris'). According to what they say in chapter 10:13, they wanted to respond to his pleas 21 days ago, but the Sar (chief, leader, ruler) of the kingdom of Persia opposed him during that time. It is not clear what this brake Gabriel could have consisted of, especially when Cyrus II was on a campaign of conquest in Central Asia.

Gabriel further adds that the arch-strategist Michael (Michael), another of the greatest archangels, had to help him, and he remained "*there with the kings of Persia* ." Although Daniel had not mentioned any apocalyptic vision immediately before, the messenger tells him, " *I have come to let you know what is to come to your people in the last days; for the vision is for those days* ." (Dan 10:14, R60) It is supposed that Gabriel speaks from a context, about the things that Daniel had seen, and now it was the moment in which they wanted to explain them in detail: «But I will declare to you what is written *in the book of truth* ..." (Dan. 10:21, R60) What he tells him about the war situation seems to be in a geopolitical context, since he announces that after finishing talking with him he must return to Miguel in the fight against the Persians , and once they have finished with them in this conflict, they will have to continue with the Greeks. This was not even something for decades later, since if this conversation was had by the angel and the prophet in the year 536 a. C., Cyrus had already taken Lydia (region of Ionia, part of the Greek territories) 10 years before, and his taking of Greece had begun with the medical wars after the death of Cyrus II and the seizure of power of Darius I. Gabriel He himself says that he was emotionally supporting Miguel in these events:

" *And I myself, in the first year of Darius the Mede, was there to encourage and strengthen him* ." (Dan. 11:1, R60)

It is strange that he mentions Darius, since at least the first Darius did not come to reign until 521 BC. C., that is, 15 years after those words. Some suggest that Darius the Mede is another person, a son of Ahasuerus, who would have been placed in control of Chaldea by Cyrus II at an advanced age:

« *History confirms the conquest of Babylon by the Persians as an event that occurred in the year 539 BC. Therefore, a theory that harmonizes the biblical account with the true historical facts is that when Cyrus conquered Babylon, being already a Persian king, he put Darius the Mede as king "...over the kingdom of the Chaldeans "(Daniel 9:1); then he had an ascension to the throne and then a "..first year.." (Daniel 9:1). Possibly, as he was 62 years old, he died of some cause, this agrees with the account of (Daniel 11:1). Thus, Darius the Mede participated in the conquest of Babylon and was coregent with Cyrus the Persian, from the year 539 a. C. until the year 537 a. C.* » (Wikipedia)

Daniel's account expresses that Gabriel anticipates the current situation and the one that would come immediately, and would trigger a takeover of the Greek kingdom, but there will be revenge for said kingdom, although it will not last long, and its power would be passed on to others:

« *Behold, there will still be three kings in Persia, and the fourth will become richer than all of them; and by making himself strong with his riches, he will raise everyone up against the kingdom of Greece.* » (Dan. 11:2, R60)

Who was he talking about? If they were under the mandate of Cyrus II, son of Cambyses I, the following rulers would be Darius I (married to Atosa, daughter of Cyrus II), later Xerxes I and then Artaxerxes I, and those who repeat this name only adding one more number, immediately following by Darius II in succession. It would seem not clear what the archangel was referring to when mentioning 3 and 4 more kings, since the Persian dynasty that came from the Achaemenids had at least 7 more successions until its end, but the truth is that he was referring to the defeat they would suffer. before " *a mighty king* " Greek who will stop them:

« *Then a mighty king will arise, who will rule with great power and do his will. But when he has risen, his kingdom will be broken and divided to the four winds of heaven; not to his descendants, nor according to the domain with which he dominated; for their kingdom will be uprooted, and it will be for others outside of them* ." (Dan. 11:3-4, R60)

How is the kingdom of this ruler of great power divided (bankrupt, broken)? Through his death, as Daniel had been told before. The angel Gabriel spoke to him about Alexander the Great. What are the "4 winds of heaven"? The 4 cardinal points. When saying that his kingdom did not pass " *to his descendants* ", nor was it " *according to the domain with which he ruled* " it is because Alexander's posthumous son (Alexander IV) was not yet of reigning age, and his fictitious appointment ended shortly after with his assassination on Cassander's orders in 310 BC. C. Even Alexander's stepbrother, Filipo III, was assassinated as well, in 317 BC. C. A legitimate son of Alexander, Heracles, was killed by Polyperchon along with his mother in 309 AD. C. Who then took power? The Council of Babylon distributes the 9 satrapies in Alexander's generals, but the general regions of control to a greater extent remain in 4 generals, one to the north, another to the south, another to the east and another to the west. It is a vision that revolves mostly in relation to the Seleucid empire, in the generals Seleucus, Cassander, Lysimachus and Ptolemy.

« *And the king of the south will become strong; but one of his princes will be stronger than him, and he will become powerful; his dominion will be great* .” (Dan. 11:5, R60)

In 323 B.C. C., after the death of Alexander, Pérdicas, one of his generals and trusted man, acting as provisional regent, appointed Ptolemy governor of Egypt and Libya, while Cassander and Lysimachus controlled the two portions of Greece (south and north, it is that is, the region of Greece that is known today, as well as southern Albania; and the region of Macedonia, which today would include almost all of Bulgaria and part of southeastern Romania), Antigonus the One-Eyed (or "the Cyclops") he controlled Asia Minor, Syria, and Judeah, and Seleucus controlled all of Babylonia, Persia, and all that came almost to India and the region of the Scythians. The idea of the wedding of Perdiccas with Cleopatra of Macedonia - sister of Alexander the Great - provoked the First War of the Deacons, led by Antipater, Craterus, Antigonus and Ptolemy, but from them, Ptolemy considered it absurd to try to take all the power, so he limited himself to consolidating the most important part of Egypt and Libya. It is possible that this is what Daniel was referring to when he spoke of the "covenant":

« *After years they will make an alliance, and the daughter of the king of the south will come to the king of the north to make peace. But she will not be able to retain the strength of her arm, nor will he remain, nor his arm; for she and those who brought her will be handed over, as will her son, and those who were on her side at that time* ." (Dan. 11:6, R60)

« *Not long after Alexander the Great died in Babylon (323 BC). After the death of his brother, several of his generals thought that they would increase their influence in Macedonia by marrying the sister of Alexander the Great. It is mentioned that Leonato was the first to ask for her hand, and he told Eumenes of Cardia that he received a promise of marriage from him. After the death of Leonato in 322 a. C., Pérdicas tried to marry her and after he died, Cassandro, Lisímaco and Antigono tried. But she refused all these offers. She escaped to Sardis, where she was captured and held in a kind of honorable captivity by Antigonus. Cleopatra eventually accepted an offer from Ptolemy I, but before she could meet him, she was captured by Antigonus and forced to return to Sardis, where she was killed in 308 BC. C., apparently by order of Antigonus, who, in any case, organized a great funeral in his honor .»* (Wikipedia)

Basically we find that he mentions the Diadocos Wars, and in its broader context almost the very Hellenistic period of Egypt, which fall within the so-called "Syrian Wars", which were a series of six armed conflicts between the Seleucid and Ptolemaic empires. during the 3rd and 2nd centuries B.C. C. on the region of Celesiria. In Ancient Egypt, at this historical stage, which succeeds the so-called Late Period, two dynasties of Hellenic origin reigned: the Macedonian (332 BC to 309 BC) and the Ptolemaic (305 BC to 30 BC). The struggles of the kingdom of the south against the kingdom of the north could include in that "north" all the rest of the other factions, not only the Diadochi, but also the generals Cassandro, Lysimachus and Antigonus I. The prophet Daniel tells us that it would be done « *strong the king of the south; but one of his princes will be stronger than him, and he will become powerful; his dominion will be great .*" (vers. 5) Who was he talking about? Quite possibly from Perdiccas, son of Orontes:

« *Before fighting against the new coalition against him, he left Eumenes of Cardia in Asia Minor, along with his brother to fight against Antipater, Craterus and Antigonus, and headed against Egypt. But his arrogance, as well as his failures before Pelusio and his attempts to cross the Nile, stirred up his soldiers. He was assassinated in 321 BC. C., in an attack carried out by two of his officers, Peitón, the satrap of Media and Seleuco I Nicator, the head of his cavalry. Seleucus gained control of Babylon and*

Syria. Perdiccas was the first of all Alexander's generals to fall. The only one of them all who died of old age and in his own bed was Ptolemy I Soter, king of Egypt .» (Wikipedia)

Perdiccas tutored the stepbrother and son of Alexander the Great, out of apparent interest in not being simply self-ruler, but legitimate heir to the throne, but also, the many intrigues and covert murders were something very seen in all these stories, including the death of the mother of the heir with the most rights to the throne, Alexander IV, who was poisoned along with his mother, Roxana, wife of Alexander the Great. Even if this interpretation were not entirely correct, comparing Daniel's quote with the events that occurred in the crisis of the Greek empire, the other episodes that follow seem to follow a very coherent sequence and similar to history. Although Cassander was behind this conspiracy, it was Seleucus who fared better in the long run:

« He had been a general in the army of Alexander the Great and two years after his death, in 321 BC. C., he was appointed satrap (governor) of Babylon and later, king of this territory, but after the defeat and death of the general Antigonus I Monophthalmos, Seleucus took control of the extensive domain that reached the present Pakistan, Iran , the mountains of India and the deserts of the Aral Sea. Of all the diadocos that divided up Alexander's empire, Seleucus was the one who took the largest part that included twenty peoples of different ethnic groups, languages and religion, and that added more than 30 million inhabitants. In the year 301 a. C. the battle of Ipsos had been fought in which Cassander of Macedonia, Lysimachus of Thrace and Seleucus fought against Antigonus Monophthalmos, the loser of the contest and who until then had taken control of the entire empire of Alexander with the intention of be the only king From that victory Seleucus reigned quietly over the extensive territory described above .» (Wikipedia)

The original Ptolemy I, named Soter, grew strong and powerful, developing Egypt beyond Alexander's wildest dreams. One of their princes, or generals, Seleucus Nicator, also became strong and powerful. And, in 312 a. C., taking advantage of the fact that Ptolemy was engaged in a war, established himself in Syria, and assumed the diadem as king. The Syrian ruler, "king of the north," was then Antiochus II, called Theos ("the divine"), and his wife was called Laodicea. According to the historian Rawlinson, " *Under her influence... he was involved in a war against Ptolemy Philadelphus [king of the south] in the year 260 BC, which ended in 252, when the marriage between Antiochus and Berenice, daughter of Ptolemy, took place.* " (A Handbook of Ancient History (Student Series), p. 251). Rawlinson says on pages 251 and 252, that « *When Philadelphus [who fathered her] died in the year 247 a. C., Antiochus repudiated Berenice and took back his former wife Laodicea, who, however, doubting his constancy, had him assassinated in order to secure the throne for his son Seleucus (II) in the year 246 BC... Laodicea had Berenice murdered .* »

From Seleuco Nicanor to Antioco I Sóter things are getting better, and every detail, every plot and every succession is fulfilled. Daniel also tells us about Antiochus, Berenice, Philadelphus and Laodice, regarding others that are coming later:

« *But a branch of his roots will rise up on his throne, and will come with an army against the king of the north, and will enter the fortress, and will do to them at will, and will prevail. And even their gods, their molten images and their precious articles of silver and gold, he will lead captive to Egypt; and for years he will stand against the king of the north. Thus the king of the south will enter the kingdom, and will return to his land. But his sons will be wrathful, and will gather a multitude of great armies; and it will come hastily and flood, and it will pass on; then he will return and take the war to his fortress. Therefore the king of the south will be enraged, and will go out and fight against the king of the north; and he will put a great multitude into the field, and all that multitude shall be delivered into his hand. And as he carries off the crowd, his heart will be lifted up, and he will strike down many thousands; but will not prevail.* » (Dan. 11:7-12, R60)

« *Ptolemy Evergetes [III, the first-born of Philadelphus and therefore Berenice's brother, branch of his roots] invaded Syria in the year 245 BC. C. with the purpose of selling the murder of his sister Berenice... In the war that broke out, he took everything he found .*» (George Rawlinson, A Handbook of Ancient History, p. 252)

A "shoot" or "branch" from its roots. Berenice's roots were her parents; therefore, the shoot would have to be his brother, who would immediately occupy the throne of the king of the south in fulfillment of this prophecy. The eighth verse of Daniel 11 says that this king of the south would take captives and objects of silver and gold to Egypt, and that his reign would continue longer than that of the king of the north, who was then Seleucus II, and verse 9 He says that he would return to Egypt. Ptolemy III fulfilled the words of verse 7, stating that " *he will come...against the king of the north, and will enter the fortress . »* And indeed he took the fortress of Syria: Seleucia (the port of Antioch) capital of the kingdom. He took with him to Egypt immense booty and 2,500 molten images and idolatrous objects, which had been taken out of Egypt in 527 B.C. C. His reign lasted until the year 222 a. C., while the king of the north, Seleucus II, died in the year 226 a. C. Seleucus II died, his two sons ruled the northern kingdom. First Seleucus III reigned for three years (226-223 BC) and then his brother Antiochus III, called "the Great", succeeded him from 223 to 187 BC. C. Both assembled immense armies to wage war against Egypt, avenge their father, and recapture the port and fortress of Seleucia (Dan. 11:10).

Antiochus the Great would have recovered the fortress of Seleucia after 27 years, and also conquered the territory of Syria up to Gaza, including Judeah. But the young Egyptian king, Ptolemy IV (Philopator), rose up, and with an army of 20,000 men dealt a heavy blow to Antiochus the Great. He killed tens of thousands and again annexed Judeah to Egypt. However, he was not strengthened because he made a sudden and hasty peace with Antiochus, and returned to a life of dissipation, wasting the fruits of victory (Dan. 11:11-12). It was « *after some years* » , exactly 12 (in 205 BC), that Ptolemy Philopator died, leaving his throne to a young son, Ptolemy Epiphanes. So Antiochus assembled a larger army and won great victories. He then concluded a treaty whereby Philip V of Macedon and others became his allies against Egypt, and together they wrested Phoenicia and southern Syria from the king of the south. In this undertaking they had the help of some Jews. The Jewish historian Josephus relates that many Jews supported Antiochus, as Daniel had announced: " *turbulent men of your people will rise to fulfill the vision, but they will fall* ." (Dan. 11:14, R60) Antiochus the Great then besieged and took Sidon from Egypt, destroyed Egyptian interests in Judeah at the Battle of Paneas (198 BCE) and then took possession of Judeah.

In the year 198 a. C. Antiochus II the Great ordered the marriage of his daughter Cleopatra I with the young Ptolemy Epiphanes, king of the south, thus subtly seeking total possession of Egypt. But the plan failed. Rawlinson says on page 254 of his work, that " *Coelesyria and Palestine, promised as dowry, were not delivered* . » In truth Cleopatra did not remain on the side of Antiochus, since it was a ruse to take Egypt, but the plan failed. Verse 18 of Daniel 11 addresses the question of how Antiochus became involved in another project: conquering the islands and coasts of Asia Minor between 197 and 196 B.C. C. However, the Roman general Lucius Cornelius Scipio [the Asian], defeated him overwhelmingly in the battle of Magnesia (190 BC).

Verse 19 tells us that Antiochus turned his attention to the strongholds of his own land, east and west. But while seeking to replace the wasted wealth looting the eastern temple of Belo in Elimais, he was killed in 187 BC. C. next, verse 20, speaks of Seleucus IV (Filopator, 187-176 BC), his son, who sent a tax collector, Heliodorus, throughout Judeah to collect money, as mentioned in 2 Maccabees 3 :21-28 and 34-36. Seleucus Philopator ruled for just 11 years, as he was poisoned by

Heliodorus. Verse 21 maintains that he left no heirs, but his brother, a younger son of Antiochus the Great, named Epiphanes (Antiochus IV), and is claimed to be a despicable reprobate, suddenly came and seized the kingdom by flattery, assisted by Eumenes. In Rawlinson's history, page 255, we read that ' *Antiochus [Epiphanes], with the help of Eumenes, overthrew Heliodorus and seized his throne in 176 B.C. C. He astonished his subjects by the affectation of his Roman-style manners* " and " *the sincere appearance of his flattery.* » This is also stated by the Hebrew sources:

« *And a despicable man will succeed him in his place, to whom they will not give the honor of the kingdom; but he will come without warning and will take the kingdom with flattery* .» (Dan. 11:21, R60)

« *Two years later, the king sent a tax collector to the cities of Judah, who appeared in Jerusalem with a mighty army. He spoke to them in a friendly way, but with the intention of deceiving them, and after gaining their confidence, he made a surprise attack on the city and dealt it a terrible blow, causing numerous casualties among the Israelites. Then he sacked the city, burned it down, and razed its houses and the wall that surrounded it. His men took the women and children prisoner and seized the cattle. Then they built a high and strong wall around the City of David, protected by mighty towers, and made it their Citadel. There they established a group of impious people, without faith and without law, who fortified themselves in that place. They supplied it with arms and food, and deposited there the booty they had gathered in the sack of Jerusalem. Thus they became a permanent threat. This became a threat to the Sanctuary, a cruel and constant hostility to Israel. They shed innocent blood around the Temple and desecrated the Holy Place. Because of them, the inhabitants of Jerusalem fled and the City became a colony of foreigners: it became strange to those who were born in it and their own children abandoned it. His Sanctuary was devastated like a desert, his festivals turned into mourning, his Saturdays into mockery and his honor into contempt. As great was his shame as his glory had been, and his greatness gave way to sorrow* . (1st Mac. 1:29-40)

Josephus and the Maccabees also tell us how Antiochus deceived the Jews through the officer in charge of domination over Jerusalem, maintaining that they deceived the Jews by telling them one thing and then doing another, to subdue and humiliate them, as other historians also mention, saying that " *He offered flattery to Eumenes, king of Pergamum, and to Attalus, his brother, and obtained their support. He offered flattery to the Romans, and sent ambassadors to court their favor, and to pay the arrears of tribute. He offered flattery to the Syrians, and won their concurrence* ." (Clarke) Regarding all this, in one of his works, the Jewish historian of the first century AD. C., Tito Flavio Josefo, mentions the following:

« *But Antiochus was not satisfied with having taken the city without his confidence, nor with having destroyed it, nor with so many deaths; before, unbridled in his vices, remembering what he had suffered in the siege of Jerusalem, he began to constrain the Jews, who rejected the custom of the homeland, not to circumcise their children, and to sacrifice pigs on the altar: to which things all contradicted and those who were good in defending this cause, were killed by them. Made Bachides captain of the garrison of the city, by Antiochus, obeying all that he had commanded, according to his natural cruelty, all wickedness exceeded, lashing one by one all the men worthy of honor, representing them every day and placing them before the eyes the prey of the city in such a way, that by the cruelty of the damages they received they were all moved to take revenge. Finally, Mattathias, son of Asamoneus, one of the priests of the place named Modin, with the people of his house (because he had five sons) took up arms and killed Bachides, and fearing the people who were in garrison, fled towards the hills. But he went down with great hope, many of the people having joined him, and fighting, defeated the captains of Antiochus, and drove them out of all the borders of Judea* ." (The Wars of the Jews. Flavio Josefo)

« *The enemy forces will be swept before him as with a flood of waters; they will be utterly destroyed, along with the prince of the covenant* ." (Dan. 11:22, R60)

The phrase " *the prince of the covenant* " is probably a reference to the high priest Onias III, who was overthrown and assassinated at this time by the deceitful maneuvers of Antiochus when he assumed power. Then, in the Spanish translation of Daniel 11:23 they write that " *after the pact with him, he will deceive and rise, and he will come out victorious with a few people* ", which is similar to the original source, but I would like to limit vocabulary issues, since more aptly it says that " *through his union with him* ", that is, a type of alliance or agreement, " *he will deceive and rise and prevail over a few people* ." So the following verses, up to 27, tell us about the failure of the attempted alliance between Antiochus and the southern kingdom, which led to a great battle that would not change the balance of power in any way.

« *When the province is at peace and in abundance, he will enter and do what his parents did not do, nor the parents of his parents; booty, spoils and riches he will distribute to his soldiers, and against the fortresses he will form his designs; and this for a while. And he will awaken his strength and his ardor against the king of the south with a great army; and the king of the south will engage in war with a large and very strong army; but he will not prevail, because they will betray him* ." (Dan. 11:24-25, R60)

Will he awaken his forces? This was accomplished when Antiochus Epiphanes led the dispute between the dynasties, but faked a friendship and alliance to catch them off guard. Despite great efforts and epic battles, Antiochus Epiphanes did not prevail, and his army was destroyed. There were two campaigns of Antiochus against Egypt, and although they were epic battles, Antiochus, returning again for a second confrontation, found that Egypt was aided by Rome, so he was forced to turn back, and in his wicked attitude, passed through Jerusalem to plunder:

« *Even those who eat of his delicacies will break him; and his army will be destroyed, and many dead will fall. The hearts of these two kings will be to do evil, and at the same table they will speak lies; but it will be of no use, because the term will not yet have arrived. And he will return to his land with great wealth, and his heart will be against the holy covenant; He will do his bidding and return to his land* ." (Dan. 11:26-28, R60)

This is believed to have been accomplished in the treason against Antiochus IV through his own advisers. The phrase in which it is stated that these kings " *sitting at the same table, will lie to each other* " , would refer to the fact that this king was not to be trusted, since he was an accomplished deceiver. It would also reveal to us that the peace tables and conferences of those times were similar to some peace tables of our time: many meetings result in treaties signed by nations, which soon become meaningless pieces of paper. Finally, verse 28 reminds us how he came against Judeah and sacked the city of Jerusalem and the holy temple, as he already referred to in the explanation of the vision of the ram and the goat. But Antiochus, wanting to come again against Egypt, is defeated:

« *At the appointed time he will return to the south; but the last coming will not be like the first. Because the ships of Quitim will come against him, and he will be saddened, and he will return, and he will be angry against the holy covenant, and he will do according to his will; therefore he will return and deal with those who forsake the holy covenant* ." (Dan. 11:29-30, R60)

Verse 30 talks about how the news that Roman ships were coming made him give up and, discouraged, he took it against Jerusalem. This came as a result of the Roman consul Gaius Popilius Lenas urging him to leave Egypt and Cyprus, so Antiochus organized an expedition against Jerusalem and sacked it. The term Quitim is Hebrew to refer to the coastal regions of southern Europe, that is, the Mediterranean, and that before the adaptation of the universalist word "Roman", it was used by the Jews to identify this town. Although the Romans are only mentioned in the Tanakh in a prophetic way, there in Daniel 11:30 and in 9:26-27: The Septuagint itself writes that a " *kingdom of the Gentiles* " will destroy the city and the holy place thus as " *the Messiah* " and then he will destroy everything " *with war* ", and it is known that this context refers to the Romans. Verse 30 of Daniel 11 is the first and only time that an explicit definition of the Romans is used, specifically in the Septuagint of the canon, translating 'Kitim' as 'Romaioi' (Romans). Antiochus launched against Jerusalem in the year 170 a. C., and at that time 100,000 Jews were killed. He eliminated the daily sacrifice that took place in the temple, and instead offered the blood and broth of a pig on the altar:

« *And troops will rise from them to desecrate the sanctuary and the fortress, and will remove the daily sacrifice, and will place the abomination of desolation. With flattery he will seduce the violators of the pact; but the people who know their God will strive and act. And the wise men of the people will instruct many; and for a few days they will fall by the sword and by fire, by captivity and by spoil. And in their fall they will be helped with little relief; and many will join them with flattery. Some of the wise will also fall to be purged and cleansed and made white, until the appointed time; because even for this there is time .*» (Dan. 11:31-35, R60)

Well, all this is already dealt with in the works of Josephus and in the books of the Maccabees, but it is very possible that quotes such as "the saints that will be purified", which appears in chapter 12, allude to these events. The events of these verses from 31 to 35 are once again the description of the abomination of destruction. The brave Maccabees tell us about all these things:

« *The king issued a decree throughout his kingdom, ordering all to form one people and renounce their own customs. All nations submitted to the king's order and many Israelites accepted official worship, offered sacrifices to idols and desecrated the Sabbath. In addition, the king sent messengers to Jerusalem and the cities of Judah, with the written order that they adopt foreign customs to the country: holocausts, sacrifices and libations should be suppressed in the Sanctuary; Saturdays and holidays were to be desecrated; the Sanctuary and the holy things had to be sullied; altars, sacred enclosures and temples to idols had to be erected, sacrificing pigs and other impure animals; boys were not to be circumcised and everyone was to make themselves abominable with all kinds of impurities and desecrations, thus forgetting the Law and changing all practices. Whoever did not act according to the king's order must die. In these terms he wrote to his entire kingdom. Furthermore, he appointed inspectors over all the people, and ordered the cities of Judah to offer sacrifices in each one of them. Many of the townspeople, all those who abandoned the Law, joined them and caused great damage to the country, forcing Israel to hide in all kinds of shelters.''*

« On the fifteenth day of the month Quisleu, in the year one hundred and forty-five, the king had the Abomination of Desolation erected on the altar of holocausts. They also built altars in all the cities of Judah. In the doors of the houses and in the squares, incense was burned. The books of the Law that were found were destroyed and thrown into the fire, and whoever was discovered with a book of the Alliance in his possession, or who observed the precepts of the Law, was sentenced to death by virtue of the decree. real. Using their strength, they continually attacked the Israelites caught in contravention in the various cities. On the twenty-fifth of each month, sacrifices were offered on the altar that stood on the altar of holocausts. Women who had circumcised their sons were killed, according to the decree, with their children hanging around their necks. The same fate suffered his relatives and all those who had participated in the circumcision. However, many Israelites stood firm and had the courage not to eat unclean food; they preferred death rather than staining themselves with that food and breaking the holy alliance, and that is why they died. And great wrath was unleashed on Israel.'' (1st Mac. 1:41-64)

It is notorious that Antiochus was a devil of his time and circumstances, especially for the Hebrew people. In his attack on Jerusalem Antiochus

IV is said to have killed 80,000 Jews, taken another 40,000 as prisoners, and sold another 40,000 into slavery. He also looted the temple, stealing around $1 billion, according to modern estimates. But now we have a problem, from verse 36 a general theory in Protestants turns, assuming that there is a jump in time to refer to the Antichrist, simply because the quotes from Daniel at this point speak of the time of the end. If so, what "end" were they talking about? The context of the theme of these events, and the end of Antiochus and his greed and tyranny, and that some of us think that it could even be really the final period that was determined on certain things, but that later was changed.

« And the king will do his will, and he will be proud, and magnify himself above all gods; and against the God of gods he will speak wonders, and prosper, until wrath is consummated; because what is determined will be fulfilled. He will not pay attention to the God of his fathers, nor to the love of women; nor will he respect any god, for he will exalt himself above all ." (Dan. 11:36-37, R60)

The word 'Elohei', translated as "god", is a generic word to refer to a deity, god or divinity, whatever the culture. The gods of the Amorites are called " *elohei haamrei* " (Judg. 6:10); the gods of the peoples mentioned, for example, in 2 Kings 18:34: *« elohei jamat ve arpad, aih elohei sproim »*... ("god of Hamat and Arfad, where is the god of Sepharvaim").

« Meanwhile, King Antiochus was touring the provinces of the plateau. There he learned that in Persia there was a city called Elimaida, famous for its riches, its silver and gold. She had a very rich temple, where gold armor, breastplates, and weapons left there by Alexander, son of Philip and king of Macedonia, the first to reign over the Greeks, were kept. Antiochus went to that city to seize it and sack it, but he did not succeed, because the inhabitants of the city, upon learning of his plans, resisted him. He had to flee and he withdrew from there very embittered to return to Babylon. While he was still in Persia, they told him that the expedition

against the country of Judah had failed. They told him that Lysias had gone at the head of a powerful army, but had had to retreat before the Jews, and that they had increased their power, thanks to the weapons and the large booty taken from the defeated armies. Furthermore, they had destroyed the Abomination that he had erected on the altar of Jerusalem and had surrounded the Sanctuary with high walls as before, doing the same with Betsur, which was one of the king's cities. " (1st Mac. 6:1-7)

The final details of these events seem generic, and may have been misinterpreted for not following a strict sequence of the above, but speaking in general. That is to say, the previous verses were talking about the Jewish situation because of Antiochus, but leave for the following verses what was happening with the power of Antiochus and the surrounding towns.

« But he will honor in his place the god of fortresses, a god that his fathers did not know; he will honor him with gold and silver, with precious stones and with things of great price. With an alien god he will make the most impregnable fortresses, and he will fill those who recognize him with honors, and for a price he will divide the land. But at the end of time the king of the south will contend with him; and the king of the north will rise up against him like a storm, with chariots and horsemen, and many ships; and it will enter through the lands, and it will overflow, and it will pass. He will enter the glorious land, and many provinces will fall; but these shall escape out of his hand: Edom and Moab, and most of the children of Ammon. He will stretch out his hand against the lands, and the land of Egypt will not escape. And he will seize the treasures of gold and silver, and all the precious things of Egypt; and those of Libya and Ethiopia will follow. But news from the east and from the north will terrify him, and he will go out in great anger to destroy and kill many. And he will plant the tents of his palace between the seas and the glorious and holy mountain; but he will come to an end, and he will have no one to help him .» (Dan. 11:38-45, R60)

« In 170 a. C., Eulao and Leneo, the two regents of the young Ptolemaic king Ptolemy VI, declared war on the Seleucid king Antiochus IV Epiphanes. In that same year, Ptolemy's younger brothers, Ptolemy VIII and Cleopatra II, were declared co-rulers in order to reinforce the unity of Egypt. Military operations did not start until 169 BC. C., when Antiochus quickly gained the initiative taking advantage of the important strategic city of Pelusio, in traditionally Egyptian territory .» (Wikipedia)

Indeed, the kingdom of the south wanted to come against the kingdom of the north in the so-called 'Sixth Syrian War', and those « *news from the east and the north* » that « *frighten it* » are, indeed, on the part of the north the Romans, and those of the east the of Mithridates I, incidents that took place shortly before the death of Antiochus Epiphanes.

" *King Mithridates I of Parthia <u>took advantage of Antiochus's western troubles and attacked from the east</u>, seizing the city of Herat in 167 BCE, disrupting the direct trade route to India, effectively dividing the Greek world in two.* **Antiochus recognized the potential danger in the east** *, but did not want to relinquish control of Judea. He sent a commander named Lysias to deal with the Maccabees, while the king himself led the main Seleucid army against the Parthians. Antiochus was initially successful in his eastern campaign, including the reoccupation of Armenia, but died suddenly of illness in 164 BC. C.* » (Wikipedia)

« Upon hearing such news, the king was dismayed, seized with a violent agitation, and fell into bed sick with sadness, because things had not turned out as he wished. He spent many days like this, unable to get rid of his melancholy, until he felt that he was going to die. Then he called all his friends and told them: "I can't sleep and I feel faint. I wonder how I got to the state of grief and bitterness in which I now find myself, I who was generous and loved while exercising the But now I realize the evils I caused in Jerusalem, when I stole the silver and gold objects that were there and I ordered the extermination of the inhabitants of Judah for no

reason. I admit that for this reason all these evils happen to me and I die of grief in a foreign land." Then he called Philip, one of his Friends, and put him in charge of his entire kingdom. He gave him his diadem, his cloak and his ring, commissioning him to direct his son Antiochus and educate him to be king. King Antiochus died in that place, in the year one hundred and forty-nine. When Lysias learned of the king's death, he put his son Antiochus, whom he had brought up from childhood, on the throne, giving him the nickname of Eupator .» (1st Mac. 6:8-17)

In conclusion, Daniel 11 begins by dealing with the matter of Greece and Persia, where Greece is to the north of both Israel and Egypt, and Persia is to the east of them all. From the apologetic and theological point of view, it must be clarified that the Persians were defeated, only the power of the northern empire remained (Macedonia, Alexander's cradle, is, by the way, the highest point of Greece). It is absurd that the editor does not clarify from the outset who are those from the "north" and the "south", as one who assumes that he is already using the conversation. Daniel, at the time, was in Persia, where his north would also be Persian, and further up the unknown Siberian regions, and Arabia to the south. Egypt is not exactly the south of Israel, although it could once be referred to as an allusion. Negeb and Teman were designations for the southern regions, but these were not to the southwest (Egypt). The southern regions of Israel and Babylon were Arabia – sometimes related to "east" -, and southern Europe was Africa. According to Strabo, the Greek term 'Aigyptos' (Egypt) meant "beyond the Aegean", that is, taking Greece as a reference, it would be the southeast.

It should be noted that this region was known as Asia in proto-Christian times, but in general its more general name was the Anatolian peninsula. The term "Anatoli" is Greek, and means "east". In the north of Israel are Turkey, Lebanon, the Balkan countries and Russia, if we are strict about the cardinal points. However, Turkey is a current country, and at the time of Daniel it belonged to the Persian empire, then it was conquered by Alexander, then by the Romans, then it was the seat of Pauline Christianity and later of Constantine, becoming the center of the empire Byzantine. After conflicts with Islam, it became a Seljuk and then absorbed the Ottoman Empire until it was divided in defeat in World War II, becoming a republic and then a government.

Verse 8 again mentions a kingdom (Egypt), where the riches are taken, where "he" would remain for years against the king of the north. Why does it say "king" of the north or south instead of saying the name of the kingdom? Because the Macedonian kingdom was divided and had not been organized since Alexander's death into a stable sovereign state; The same happened with Egypt, with the syncretism of the Ptolemaic dynasty. On top of this, they were both part of the same Greek domain, only they were at odds within an internal personal conflict, the northern faction and the southern faction. This type of conflict with Egypt and the Hellenes is even mentioned among the Maccabean texts, since the Jews participated on a couple of occasions in these combats (eg Dan. 11:14). In the end, Egypt could not hold its own against the Greek power of the north and the east, not even with alliances with royal women and with large armies, and they betray it. Later Rome (Kittim) begins to take power and from them comes sovereignty over the entire Old World, and they annex Egypt and control it. Before starting the devastating abomination, Antiochus was preparing his Second Expedition against Egypt, where he would be threatened by the Romans and that would be when he would take it on with the Jews.

*About this time Antiochus **was preparing his second expedition against** Egypt . And it happened that for about 40 days there appeared throughout the city, running through the air, horsemen dressed in gold, armed troops divided into squads, drawn swords, cavalry regiments in battle order, attacks and raids from both sides. , movements of shields, clouds of spears, shots of arrows, flashes of gold fittings and armor of all* *kinds. Given this, everyone prayed that this apparition was a sign of good omen.* » (2nd Mac. 5:1-4)

Then, after the warning of the Roman consul Gaius Popilius Lenas, about leaving Egypt and Cyprus, the desolating abomination takes place, when Antiochus IV's greed and frustration make him seek some comfort and a place with low defenses. Alexander's kingdom was divided towards the "4 winds of heaven", that is, the cardinal points, but not from Israel (because Alexander was not a Jew but a Macedonian), but from Greece: that is, in the strict sense, taking as references the Hellenic Empire of Alexander. Although, the old world was not distributed in a homogeneous and symmetrical way, so there could be more kingdoms to the north and none to the south (to give an example), so it is a way of saying that the kingdom was distributed "to all parts", as seen in the north with Cassander, in the south with Ptolemy, to Anatolia went Lysimachus, and further to the east Seleucus. Verse 31 narrates the capture of Jerusalem and its desecration in the days of the Maccabees, when the priestly services and sacrifices stopped, and when the descendants of Seleucus had also controlled that location. The text then talks about the end of the reign of those 4 kings (Alexander's generals: Seleucus, Ptolemy, Cassander and Lysimachus), when their evil was completed or concluded, and where another superior "melej" (king) appeared. Melech is both king in the singular and the idea of a kingdom or system of government.

It is notorious that after the dissolution and fall of the Hellenic forces, it was Rome that took power until today, not only in that region but in the entire world. That first king that I assume you are talking about, will be where the destroyers of Judeah (the people of the saints) would come from and who would expel the Jews from their land. The vision with the Medical Wars (between the Achaemenid Empire and the Hellenic city-states), began around 490 BC. C. and later came the revenge of Alexandro (Alexandros, Alejandro), and his succession. Not everything Daniel said had to do with the Maccabees, but with the geopolitical situation around them. Daniel 8 incorporates into the revelation the events during the history of the Maccabees, even from before the birth of Mattathias the Hasmonean, and Daniel 11 does address the issue, first indirectly, and then directly. Consequently, the subject of the Maccabees is the subject of Daniel 11, not of the rest of the visions that the prophet had, although they were part of an aspect of historical synchronicity, such as chapter 8. For all this, I recommend reading these works to better understand the matter of Daniel chapter 11.

Egypt was forcibly Hellenized until 30 B.C. C., at the time of Cleopatra and Marco Antonio. Egypt progressively left Hellenism , absorbing some Judaism into its national ideas, and then Christianity, which grew stronger making Egypt a Christian nation until 6 centuries later, when Muhammad's forces invaded Egypt. Some believe that the southern kingdom was the Muslims, but as we can compare with the facts and quotes, that assumption is incorrect. Furthermore, Islam came neither from the north nor from the south, but from Arabia, to the east (in fact, the term Arab means "east"). For example, Turkey itself, then known by other names, depending on the era and empire, had no part in the relevant issues of the history of the Assyrian, Babylonian, Persian, Hellenic, and Roman powers. It wasn't until the Seljuk Empire, in the 10th century. South of the Seljuk Empire there was nothing relevant to the story given to Daniel or anything to do with the Jews. What they narrated to Daniel was regarding the nations around Israel until the Jews were expelled in AD 135. C. The events from there, until the return of the State of Israel, in 1948, are ephemeral and strictly generic.

VIII. THE SEALED PROPHECY

As if chapter 11 were not explanatory and extensive enough, chapter 12 seems to continue to address the matter, but making it seem as if it were talking about the end times. The point is that we forget that there were at least 400 years from the days of Daniel to the time of Antiochus IV, and that is said soon and fast, but even for us to imagine 400 years ahead is beyond our capabilities, and to look back 400 It would be to refer us to the Middle Ages, that is, a completely different time, without a point of comparison. It is understandable then that it was logical that they told Daniel that these things were "future" and related to another "epoch", part of a "coming era", one that, due to its future context, belonged to the end of time:

" *And at that time Mikael will rise, the great ruler who stands over the sons of your people ...*" (Dan. 12:1)

By saying "that time", it is a context of "back then", that is, in that other time, in the future. It does not mean that it was just in the days of Antiochus, but in the "future age" in which all these things would happen - although for us they have already happened. The key point with this is the core of the dialogue, what are they trying to convey and what is the goal with so many words? It all came from Daniel and the concern he had for his people and the hope they held. They awaited the redemption of their people, the reign of the Messiah and the resurrection of the dead, and Gabriel indicated the things that should precede those episodes, that is, the prelude that would present the circumstances for the redemption of Israel to arrive with the utopian era under the leadership of the Messiah. So what did the future hold before that? Since Daniel, even the fall of the empire that was still in power (Babylon), and that had taken Judah captive; the subsequent fall of the empire that would in turn destroy it (Persia), followed by the one that would subdue it (Macedonia). Then, the Roman empire would come, with whom another history would follow, one much more lasting than the previous ones, and which would begin almost at the time of the first appearance of the Messiah, and would end giving rise to the empire that would be ended by the second coming of the Messiah. Understanding this, the syntax and dialogue between these two personalities is coherent:

«... it will be a time of anguish, which never was since there were people until then; but at that time your people will be released, all those who are found written in the book .» (Dan 12:1, R60)

It would not be crazy to assume that this description heralds the apocalyptic Great Tribulation, and agrees with many other prophecies, but it does state that "his people" would be "delivered" (delivered, redeemed, rescued). Has that already happened? When referring to his people, he adds something that seems to assume that they are « *all those found written in the book* », but what book? If we carry out a prophetic synchronization, it seems that it describes the "chosen ones", those of whom Jesus Christ also mentions. Would this then be an allusion to the great Tribulation and Rapture? Well, the thing is that Daniel 12:1, by saying in Hebrew, « *vebaet hahia* » (and in time the one), means, "in that future", not "in that moment", explicitly. That is why the Jewish sages translated into the Septuagint that « *at the appointed time* » , after those things, would be when Michael would appear. In other words, first there would be the expulsion of the Jews and 1,900 years of deportation, and when they returned, the time of Israel would come again, since before that " *the times of the Gentiles* " had to pass (Luke 21:24), which were to be fulfilled. . Yeshua spoke of that time when it would still be the domination of the Gentiles, and even Daniel refers to it in the same verse 1, when he says "Goi" (nations, Gentiles, people).

" *And many of those who sleep in the dust of the earth will be awakened, some to eternal life, and others to shame and perpetual confusion .*" (Dan 12:2, R60)

According to Christian eschatology, the Rapture is part of the First Resurrection, and consequently, this "time" in which Michael rises is precisely the Apocalypse, marked by the great Tribulation, the sign from heaven (the fight between Michael and the Dragon) which precedes the Rapture, and which is almost simultaneous with that part of the First Resurrection described in the book of John on Patmos. If we could therefore improve the semantics and syntax of these passages to facilitate our current understanding of the facts, we would say that Gabriel makes it clear to him that what Daniel expected of his people (that really for God they are the elect, not just the people of meat) was to take place after these Babylonian, Persian and Greek wars, when the Roman power came. However, it is still strange that when the Roman Empire arrived there were no prophecies about them, as with the previous ones, to know how long their domination would last and how it would end.

Ergo, yes there is, but it is not in the biblical canon for various reasons, for example, the Sibylline Oracles mention this, but who would include a book by a Greek fortune teller in the canon? The 2nd book of Esdras talks about this, but Martin Luther did not accept this version, which did appear in the Vulgate version of Jerome, and which was part of the original Tanakh. And what with 2nd Baruc? This already seems a bit more apocryphal, that is, a bit darker and more mystical, since this type of writing was part of the inter-testamental period, and consequently, it was debatable to what degree it should be incorporated into the Tanaj canon. . Even so, these texts were found in the Qumran caves as part of the Jewish historicity, and in their case it seems clear that the angel of Iaheveh commanded Ezra that only 24 books were part of the sacred compendium, while the other 70 - between those who were possibly 2nd Baruc - were only part of the study of the wise. Apart from these, there are more sources, and they expose us to the history and metamorphosis of the dark Roman Empire to get to prepare the kingdom of the Antichrist, which is the gateway to the last phase of the end of this era, which we traditionally call, Apocalypse.

« Those who understand will shine like the brightness of the firmament; and those who teach justice to the multitude, like the stars for ever and ever. But you, Daniel, shut up the words and seal the book until the time of the end. Many will run from here to there, and knowledge will increase
." (Dan. 12:3-4, R60)

This verse 3 is notorious as it anticipates the millennial era of the Messiah, evidently after these events and "the cherry on the cake": the last of the last, or the beginning of a new era. What it basically exposes is that the end times was a "sealed" information that would not yet be revealed, but would be made known and its patterns would begin to unleash once the vision of the devastating abomination had been fulfilled. Daniel was informed of what was relevant until the appearance of the Messiah and the New Covenant, as he clarifies at the end of chapter 9, but from then on, it would be John, the apostle of Jesus Christ, who would reveal what encompasses the next phase of events (without have other individuals who would prophesy and predict within the period of Roman rule). It must be clarified that by saying "Roman rule" I am not referring to Italy or the Vatican, but to the shadow power that governs the world and that has come through the Roman Empire until today to control the planet.

Daniel is told to "stop the words" until then, that is, the message (what he has been told), and seal the "book" until the time of the end. It is evident that if Daniel died about the sixth century B.C. C., he could not be sealing the book until the end. Something is not sealed daily, but something is written and sealed until the moment it must be opened. The seals were signs stamped to protect the confidentiality of information, and could not be uncovered until it reached the hands of its recipient or the time it was broken. What I mean is that the text does not say that these words are "closed and sealed", but that Daniel is told of a " *closing of the words* ", and that he " *stops the message* ". When saying "ha.dbarim", it is translated as "the words" or "the things", regarding the message itself, and, apart, "seal the book". To seal something was to leave it under a stamp, to leave it covered, to finish a subject or to reserve information until the moment that corresponds to be released. I believe that Daniel only knew details, like the other prophets and apostles, but not the context of the events. In other words, that information was "classified" until the year 90 AD, when God Himself made it known to Jesus, and then Yeshua revealed it to an appointed angel and he revealed it to John on Patmos (Rev. 1:1)..

Assuming this, Paul could not know this, also assuming that John was the last of the apostles left alive and that Paul's letters were written about 20 to 30 years from the Lord, that is, with an interval of about 30 or 40 years before the revelation of John. By saying "seal the vision and prophecy", she clarifies that it is "sealed", not that it opens - as some tend to interpret -, but in the Hebrew ideology, "sealing" is also "determining", and as other passages reflect and the whole context, it is determined what will be done for the end and on the devastating (Rome, which will be the last empire that will remain), and after more than 600 years it is explained to Juan. The seals are opened in the vision, showing the future, but the events will actually occur later. So, of all that he was told, what was sealed until it was opened (known) at the time of the end? They tell him that " *many will run (will be in a hurry) and knowledge will increase* ."

Since it is a context, it is understood that the time of the end and this phrase of the "rush" and the increase of the "scientific" (or "advancement") are related. Everything that was revealed to Daniel ended with the 'Et' (time, period) of the abomination of desolation, which – by the way – is later than the other 'Et' (defined as 'Ketz' (conclusion, completion).), and they do add further information there, telling him that there were 1,290 days and another 45 with respect to that 'Et' that he had previously been told about (chapters 8 and 11). In other words, despite the fact that they couldn't tell him more, they did add to him about the last thing he was temporarily allowed to know: the devastating abomination referred to explicitly shortly before. Because? Because the revelations about the end times have been kept hidden and encrypted so that the forces of evil do not try to avoid their own destiny (this is a little more difficult to explain and it is time to get into quantum physics (theory of Relativity). of Time, or "times", and its "variables" within the destination), but in order not to get off topic I will leave it there).

We see that Daniel had many important visions throughout his life, although one reads them in a couple of chapters as if they were something correlative that he received in just a few days. Chapter 12 is one of those visions, and it represents the end of a series of many visions throughout her life, but especially the outcome of what was referred to in chapter 11, and in the long term after chapter 9. So, from everything they told him, at that point they are talking about, they tell him that "*many will run (will be in a hurry) many and knowledge will increase* ."

Basically Daniel received coded "information packets" of future events, some more secret than others, and those relating to 'Et Ketz' were totally unknown until they were revealed to John on Patmos. There were only isolated comments like a puzzle with many pieces that only have a few known and scattered. Why only until Juan? Because the words of the previous 'Et' (period, time) had already been fulfilled: the Messiah and the devastating abomination. If the Messiah did not do his part, this new "information package" could not be fulfilled. Since the Messiah fulfilled his part (most of the 70 conspiracies, especially aimed at the spiritual liberation of man), it was possible to proceed to the expected end. This is what the Jews who await a different Messiah than Yeshua still do not understand: without first saving the soul, a military salvation is useless. The "time of the end" is a context. In Hebrew there are several words for "time", and each one has an explicit meaning that, even if it is translated, does not mean that it is the same as what is understood in Spanish. For example, we say, "the era of the Renaissance", but that era is not rounded decimals, but goes from a certain period of the fifteenth century to a certain moment of the sixteenth century.

As for the history of Israel, since the nation dissolved in 720 B.C. C. (although they had already divided in 930 BC), the eschatological context revolved around the return of the tribes and the reunification and return of the power of the people of Israel, and their glorification as in Solomon's time. That, according to their understanding and culture, was prophesied, but it would occur as a prelude to the era of peace of the Messiah. Therefore, everything related to this context was a matter of the "period of the end", not because everything ends, but that the dispersion of the people of Israel ends and the era begins (period, era, aeon, generations, etc.) of the Messiah. Consequently, the "time of the end" is a very long period of time that has within it sub-periods (different groups of events and developments). This vision is part of the visions of the end times, although for us they are already past time. In a global sense, from Abraham to today, many visions developed, but there was a, let's call it, "blueprint" to finalize certain things and bring about peace and justice. For this there were a series of things that had to happen, and this was being made known through visions: some have already happened and others have yet to happen.

For example, this vision is explained to Daniel, and he says, " *Behold, I will show you what is to come after the indignation, because [it is] for [the] final period .*" (Ch. 8:19) What indignation? The indignation is the event prior to what Gabriel is going to explain to him, and what he is going to explain is relative to the "appointed time" or "end time" for the final events: this can be a very long period of time and of diverse visions within. The events with Antiochus would be a package of events for a pattern of the end times, at the beginning, only that for us that is already past, even the very distant past. Now, continuing with the dynamic:

" *And I, Daniel, looked, and behold, two others stood, one on this side of the river, and the other on the other side of the river. And one said to the man dressed in linen, who was on the waters of the river: When will be the end of these wonders? And I heard the man dressed in linen, who was on the waters of the river, who raised his right hand and his left hand to heaven, and swore by him who lives forever, that it will be for time, times, and half a time. . And when the dispersion of the power of the holy people is finished, all these things will be fulfilled ."* (Dan. 12:5-7, R60)

Wonders? Yes, for us they were things of past peoples, but if we remove these precedents, and all that hit us suddenly, being something completely new, it would impact us greatly. When saying this to Daniel, who lived in the dispersion, he does not understand it, and if he had believed he understood it, he would have interpreted that the return of his people would be the end of time. However, it did not make much sense, because there was no context for that to take place, since the 10 tribes were in Assyria, and what power was going to make the 10 tribes return from Assyria, and more when they had been living there for more? 150 years? That was possible thanks to the United Nations partition decree of 1947 for the misnamed territory of "Palestine". Daniel, how was I supposed to know all this? Many things still had to happen and he was only informed of the events until the Messiah and the devastating abomination that the Romans brought, and even that he is not said to have known how to interpret or understand. That is why he asks and they answer him that it is closed and sealed until the end time. In other words, it was not up to him to know them, but they do give him some brushstrokes.

You have to know how to correctly separate verse 7, because it has two parts, 1st, it talks about the end of those events from there back (that is, the visions of chapter 11, and its context with 8) and 2nd, it is about the signal to complete this set of prophecies. In other words, all these things that Daniel saw would be accompanied by others beyond those seen at the end of chapter 9, and that would fulfill the total time that had to elapse until the other stage of the "time of the end" arrived, which would begin when " *the dispersion of the power of the holy people* " ended . Ergo, when is the end of these things? What things? What were they talking about there? There, each one of his visions is not being treated, but that [vers. 1] Michael will rise (a euphemism to refer to a military uprising) and there will be great tribulation, [vers. 2] many will be raised from the dead, and [vers. 3] the righteous will shine (euphemism to refer to stand out, understand and be glorified). That is the "end" of those wonderful things that were told to Daniel and about which he wanted to know more, of which "one" asks (vers. 6), and they answer him: "when the dispersion of the power of *the holy people, all these things will be accomplished* ." (Dan 12:7, R60)

Holy people? Some theologians interpret that the "holy people" were people from the time of Yeshua, or the Christians. Others say that they are non-carnal people, that is, resurrected people. The text does not say that they are carnal or that they are not carnal. The word "holy", depending on the context, does not have to be explicitly "holy" people in the sense of immaculate, but "consecrated": people "dedicated" or on the way to "sanctification" for an objective, service or role. According to the history of Israel, they were called for this (regardless of the fact that the majority of the people were not suitable or accepted their call). The writing does not say "children of God", as others assume, but "holy people". These are two different things, and what unites them is a context for the time of the end, when the true Israel will be raised up by Messiah, removing the unclean from Israel, and adding to Israel the saints from the Gentiles, to create one town.

Now, if we could compartmentalize the visions of the end times, the first group would be the wars of Babylon with Persia; the second group those of Persians and Greeks; the third of the Greeks in their own interior, including the struggles of their northern and eastern part against the southern part (Egypt); the fourth, the rise of the Roman empire with the coming of the Messiah and the New Covenant, but also the destruction of Jewish identity; the fifth the age of Pisces under Roman rule; the sixth, the arrival of the New World Order (born with the establishment of the United Nations Organization, in 1947), which is when the holy people return (1948, when the end of the "times of the Gentiles" begins, marked by the First and Second World War) and their power (1967), and recover their city (Jerusalem) so that what was said by the prophet Zechariah (1973) can be fulfilled. More, when did the Dispersion end for these things to be fulfilled? In 1948, after the Jews officially returned to the State of Israel. From here, as the rest of the prophecies of the holy prophets point out, the period of the end times begins, when Israel recovers its "power" and the end of the "times of the Gentiles" begins.

In the Six Day Wars they showed that they once again had divine backing and the autonomy to fend for themselves against their enemies, but this was fully evident in the Yom Kippur War, showing the world that Israel was one of the half dozen of nations on the planet that possessed nuclear weapons. Some have translated here, in Daniel, "dispersion", because it is difficult to translate a book wanting to be concise and subject to being literal or interpreting. In itself, what it refers to is that these things will begin to be fulfilled when the people of Israel return from their dispersion and recover their strength. For our culture – as seen at a historical level – we Jews lost our power when the tribes divided, and since then only in isolated moments did we have any kind of strength as a people, in regards to our enemies or the rest of the nations. In 1948 we returned to our nation after thousands of years of disintegration and expatriation, as the prophets had said (especially Isaiah, Joel and Jeremiah), in 1967 the first show of union of strength of the Jewish people was manifested, but in 1973, the Jewish people , as a united and strong nation, stood up to its enemies and the surrounding nations, and began to be recognized militarily worldwide. Israel had lost this since the days of David and Solomon, and was guilty of the empires of the Gentiles.

The Hebrew euphemism " *iad-am-kedesh* " refers to the strength and power of the people of Israel, the strength as a nation, understood to stand up to other nations. Kedesh is not saying that they are holy, but rather that they are a consecrated people, as Peter (1st Pe. 2:9) rightly wrote, a Jew, who was speaking of us, not of the Gentiles. When Daniel wanted to know about the future, they told him that it was "sealed" until the time of the end, and regarding this they told him, in a few words, that his work ended there, that he would rest and be with his ancestors and in the future would receive its due. Daniel is the most important prophet regarding "the future history of the past", but his role only lasted until the information concerning the birth of the Roman empire, and what follows from there – and this is history – was revealed to John Jr. of Zebedee on Patmos. Daniel's contextual visions end in time for the time of the work of the Messiah and the abomination of desolation, and at that time the following is made known only to John, and not as any revelation, but as something that had effectively been sealed. (with 7 seals, to be more exact), and that it was only made known by God himself (he gave it to Yeshua, Yeshua to one of his angels, and this angel revealed it to John).

« And I heard, but I did not understand. And I said: My Lord, what will be the end of these things? He replied: Go, Daniel, for these words are closed and sealed until the time of the end. Many will be clean, and made white, and purified; the wicked will do wickedly, and none of the wicked will understand, but the wise will understand ." (Dan. 12:8-10, R60)

Here we have another part that we must separate, since in translation and mere linear interpretation everything seems the same, but it is not. Verse 10 fits perfectly with the Maccabean story, rather than future things that might seem generic about the elect.

*« <u>The women who had circumcised their children were killed</u> , according to the decree, with their children hanging around their necks. <u>The same fate suffered his relatives and all those who had participated in the circumcision.</u> However, **many Israelites stood firm and had the courage not to eat unclean food; they preferred death rather than staining themselves with that food and breaking the holy alliance, and that**

is why they died . *And great wrath was unleashed on Israel* ." (1st Mac. 1:60-64)

Mattathias *answered in a loud voice: "Even if all the nations under the king's rule obey and abandon the worship of their ancestors to submit to his orders, I, my sons and my brothers will remain faithful to the Covenant of our* **fathers** . <u>*Heaven free us from abandoning the Law and the precepts.*</u> *We* **will not abide by the king's orders by deviating from our worship, neither to the right nor to the left** ." *When he had finished pronouncing these words, a Jew stepped forward in full view to offer a sacrifice on the altar of Modin, according to the king's decree. Seeing this, Mattathias was inflamed with zeal and his insides trembled; and being carried away by a righteous indignation, he pounced and slew his throat on the altar. Right there he killed the royal delegate who forced the sacrifices to be offered and destroyed the altar. Thus he manifested his zeal for the Law, as Pinchas had done with Zimri, son of Salu. Then he began to shout through the city with all his might: "Everyone who is zealous for the Law and wants to stay true to the Alliance, follow me." And abandoning all that they possessed in the city, he and his sons fled to the mountains* ."

« <u>*Then many Jews, lovers of justice and rights, withdrew into the desert to settle there with their wives, their children and their cattle, because misfortune had been unleashed on them*</u> . *The king's officials and the garrison residing in Jerusalem, in the City of David, received the complaint that some men, violating the king's order, had gone to hide in the hiding places of the desert. A strong contingent went out to pursue them and managed to catch up with them. They surrounded them and prepared to attack them. It was a Saturday, and they were told: "It is time to end this! Come out, carry out the king's order and you will save your lives!"* *They replied:* **"We will not go out, nor will we obey the royal order, thus desecrating the Sabbath."** *They immediately attacked them, but* **they did not fight back, not even throwing stones at them or closing the entrance to their shelters. "Let's all die, they said, maintaining our integrity** . *Heaven and earth are witnesses that you make us perish* *unjustly." Thus they were attacked in the middle of the Sabbath, and the men perished with their wives, their children, and their cattle. There were a total of about a thousand people*." (1st Mac. 2:19-38)

Now comes the end of this chapter, with a denouement that explains the above and everything that it encompasses, especially regarding the neuralgic issue of the matter: the devastating abomination of Antiochus IV.

« *And from the time that the continuous sacrifice is removed until the abomination of desolation, there will be one thousand two hundred and ninety days. Blessed is he who waits, and reaches one thousand three hundred and thirty-five days. And you will go to the end, and you will rest, and you will rise to receive your inheritance at the end of the days*." (Dan. 12:11-13, R60)

Daniel 12:11 is mistranslated. It does not say "And from the time the daily sacrifice is removed until the abomination of desolation..." If not, " from *the time the daily [sacrifice] is removed and the abomination of desolation is given [it will be] 1290 days* . » That is to say, they are two things that occurred at the same time, because since the nonsense of Antiochus began by prohibiting the liturgy and religious services in Judeah together with the desecration of the sanctuary, until the city and the town were liberated and the sanctuary was sanctified again, 3 and a half years elapsed. There is no Hebrew or Aramaic term that defines "continual sacrifice", it is an idea that stems from the word Tamid. The word Tamid refers to something "continuous", continuously. For example "anshéi tamíd" (men with constant responsibility), or "esh tamíd" (fire that burns permanently) or "arruját tamíd" (continuous ration). The ha-tamid form is interpreted as "minját tamíd" (continuous sacrifice), but beware, that is an interpretation, since it only says "ha-tamid" (continuous, habitual, constant). This is how this Hebrew form is used in the Aramaic references to Daniel (chs. 8:11-13, 11:31 and 12:11). That means that the word "UNTIL" is an addition of the translator, and what he is affirming is that it is the same period in which the Tamid and the Shkutz Shmem take place. The Tamid is first and then the Skutz Shmem, one immediately followed by the other, that is, the religious services cease and the desolation begins, one with the other, and all this lasts 1,290 days in its entirety until death and the Temple are destroyed. hallowed.

The inhabitants of Jerusalem were affected and services had been canceled in the temple by decree of Antiochus IV, and were not resumed until the Dedication (which is commemorated on the festival of Chanukah). In any case, the factor of those days is repeated, because the value of 7 and its two halves (3 ½ + 3 ½) is a key time sequence or pattern in development processes. For example, the fact that there is an analogy between the 3 and a half years of abomination in Jerusalem and the 3 and a half years of the power of the Antichrist is because there is a time pattern related to the number 7 and its half (3 and a half), as also Jonah was in the supposed fish 3 days and 3 nights, or the Lord was in Hades 3 days and 3 nights (actually 3 and a half, ranging from the afternoon of a Yom Rebií (Wednesday) to the dawn of a Yom Rishon (Sunday), or 3 and a half days that the bodies of Enoch and Elijah will be left unburied in Jerusalem.

Ergo, then he adds that " *fortunate is the one who waits and reaches the day 1335* " , that is, resists 45 more days after the conclusion of the 1290 (3 and a half years). The sacrifices ceased at the same time that the abomination of desolation began (the siege of Jerusalem and the destruction of the temple). That is why the 42 months are 3 and a half years, but not 1260, but 1290 days. The idea of "time, times and half a time" and similar values do not refer to a single date but to a basic pattern that repeats itself because it represents half a cycle of time. Those who held out for 45 days, longer than the time that Antiochus IV's abomination lasted, were definitively freed. By Antiochus IV the services were suspended, since he prohibited them, and by Titus, because when attacking the temple, everything was destroyed and the ritual religious practice of the priests ceased.

« In what way Antiochus, called Epiphanes, having won Jerusalem, and having held it for three years and six months under his rule, was driven out of it by the sons of Asamoneus ...»

" The princes of the Jews were at variance among themselves at the time that Antiochus, called Epiphanes, contended with Ptolemy the Sixth over the Empire of Syria, which he coveted so much, whose quarrel was over dominion, because each of them, being honored and powerful, considered it a serious thing to suffer subjection from his peers; Onias, one of the high priests, prevailing over the others, drove the sons of Tobias out of the city. These then came to Antiochus, very humble begging him to arm an army against Judea, that they would guide him. And because the king himself was very eager for this business, he readily consented to what they begged. In such a way that with many soldiers he went out to continue the company; and after having fought the city with great force, he took it, and killed a multitude of Ptolemy's friends; and giving license to his own to sack the city, he himself robbed the entire temple, and forbade the continuation of daily religion for a period of three years and six months .»
(The Wars of the Jews, Tito Flavio Josefo)

" And troops will rise from him to desecrate the sanctuary and the fortress, and will remove the daily sacrifice, and will put the abomination of desolation ." (Dan. 11:31, R60)

IX. THE CONFUSION OF THE ESCHATOLOGICAL SERMON

« *Seeing Pilate that nothing advanced, but that more riot was made, he took water and washed his hands in front of the people, saying: I am innocent of the blood of this just man; there you. And answering all the people, said:* **His blood be on us, and on our children** . » (Matt. 27:24-25, R60)

He who kills another "loads his blood on him", that is, the guilt of being murdered, and he who kills with iron dies, because what you sow, you reap. Not 30 years had passed since that incident, when Vespasian annihilated those people through his son Titus. The supposed "revenge" on the Jewish people (Luke 21:23) because of participating in the conspiracy to kill Yeshua would be a logical answer to why this misfortune occurred on the Jews: Every action has its consequence, and Jerusalem he paid for what he did, as Jesus had prophesied. The synoptic gospels, and other parabiblical ones, tell us that Yeshua had a conversation with his followers regarding an "abomination of desolation" that the prophet Daniel had spoken of. We have seen that Daniel 11:31 and 12:11 mention an "abomination of desolation", but would that be what Yeshua was referring to? The Septuagint writes in Greek, in the cases of Daniel, « *bdéligma erimóseos* » and « *bdélima tis erimóseos* », respectively, and in the later revision or « *bdéligma ifanisménon* » and « *bdéligma erimóseos* » . This also appears in the case of Matthew 24:15 and Mark 13:14, but Luke's explanation differs here, and instead of saying " *bdéligma tis erimóseos* " , he writes what translated into RVA 60 is:

" *But when you see Jerusalem surrounded by armies, then know that its destruction has come* ." (Luke 21:20, R60)

It is not possible that Yeshua was talking about the same thing as Daniel 11:31 and 12:11. To begin with, what Daniel said there had happened almost 190 years before, and also here there was talk of a siege of Jerusalem, since Antiochus IV did not besiege the city under those canons. The siege of Jerusalem took place 30 years after the words that Yeshua was referring to his followers, as he himself said:

« *As Jesus left the temple and was leaving, his disciples came up to show him the buildings of the temple. Answering him, he said to them: Do you see all this? Truly I tell you, <u>not a stone will be left here on a stone that will not be thrown down</u>* ." (Matt. 24:1-2, R60)

That same day, before entering the city, he himself had already spoken sadly words of sadness about the near future of Jerusalem:

« *And when he came close to the city, seeing it, he wept over it, saying: Oh, if you also knew, at least on this your day, what is for your peace! But now they are hidden from your eyes. For the days will come upon you, when **your enemies will surround you with a fence, and besiege you, and will close you in on all sides, and will bring you down to the ground, and your children within you, and will not leave one stone upon another in you, because you do** not You knew the time of your visitation* ." (Luke 19:41-44, R60)

It is notorious that Yeshua was not referring to the devastating abomination of Antiochus IV, nor to something very distant in time, since his words explain everything by themselves:

«*... those who are in Judea, flee to the mountains. Let him who is on the roof not come down to take something from his house; and let him who is in the field not turn back to take his cloak. But woe to those who are pregnant, and to those who give birth in those days! Pray therefore that your flight may not be in winter or on a Sabbath day ...*" (Matt. 24:16-20, R60)

« *But when you see the desolating abomination of which the prophet Daniel spoke, placed where it should not be (he who reads, understand), then those who are in Judea flee to the mountains. Let him who is on the housetop not go down into the house, nor go in to take anything from his house; and let him who is in the field not return back to take his cloak. But*

*woe to those who are pregnant, and to those who give birth in those days!
Pray therefore that your flight may not be in winter ..."* (Mar. 13:14-18,
R60)

*« Then those who are in Judea, flee to the mountains; and those who are
in the midst of it, leave; and those who are in the fields, do not enter it.
Because* **_these are days of retribution_** *, so that all things that are written
may be fulfilled. But woe to those who are pregnant, and to those who
give birth in those days! for there will be great calamity on the earth, and
wrath on this people. And they will fall by the edge of the sword, and* **will
be led captive to all nations** *; and Jerusalem will be trodden down by
the Gentiles, until the times of the Gentiles are fulfilled ."* (Luke 21:21-24,
KJV 60)

Those words evoked a prophecy already known, and that had not yet
been fulfilled. Josephus later recalled her, when he narrated:

*« When those who remained alive were so terrified, the dead seemed to
have reached more rest than the living, and more bliss; And those who
were imprisoned, considering the torments they suffered, considered those
who were dead and unburied to be much happier than themselves: they
violated all rights of men, they laughed at God and his things; They made
fun of the prophets and what they had prophesied, no less than if they
were fabulous answers. Having, then, already disregarded all the laws and
ordinances that their ancestors had made in matters pertaining to virtue,
they verified with experience* **_what had long before been prophesied
of Jerusalem: there was among them that ancient prophecy that the
city had of being prey, and that their holy laws and sacred things, had
to be burned by law of war,_** *making revolt and sedition among them
, having themselves first soiled and violated the temple with their own
hands. The Zealots wanted to show themselves ministers and executors of
these things, as men who had no doubts about it ."* (The Wars of the Jews.
Book V. Chapter 2).

« *Is Israel a servant? Is he a slave? Why has he come to be prey? The lion's cubs roared against him, lifted up their voice, and laid waste his land; Their cities are burned, without an inhabitant.*" (Jeremiah 2:14-15, R60)

« *The plant that your right hand planted, and the renewal that you affirmed for yourself. It is burned by fire, devastated; They perish from the rebuke of your face* ." (Psalm 80:15-16, R60)

« *The house of the wicked will be laid waste; But flourish tent of the upright. There is a path that seems right to man; But its end is the way of death* ." (Proverbs 14:11-12, R60)

« *Your land is destroyed, your cities set on fire, your land before you eaten by foreigners, and desolate as desolation of strangers. And the daughter of Zion remains as a branch in a vineyard, and as a cabin in a melon grove, as a devastated city. If Yaheveh Tzabaot had not left us a small remnant, we would be like Sodom, and similar to Gomorrah* ." (Isaiah 1:7-9, R60)

« *And say to the people of the land: Thus has Yaheveh Adonai said about the inhabitants of Jerusalem and about the land of Israel: Their bread they will eat with fear, and with fear they will drink their water; for his land will be deprived of its fullness, because of the wickedness of all who dwell in it. And the inhabited cities will be deserted, and the land will be desolate; and you will know that I am Yaheveh* ." (Ezekiel 12:19-20, R60)

Some will assume that these prophecies referred to the Assyrian captivity or the Babylonian deportation, but the truth is that neither of those episodes left the land of Israel barren and abandoned (even Nebuchadnezzar left the peasants and farmers in Judeah so that the land would not be dry). and wasteland).

Let's see the points that lead to the confusion of this whole subject. In most Christian theological interpretations, these quotes are a purely eschatological matter, that is, they belong to something that has yet to take place, not something that has already happened. First of all, these specific words of Yeshua in the eschatological sermon do not fit with the current situation in Jerusalem. Can anyone imagine what would happen to the Jews if they "fled to the mountains" today? Jerusalem today is surrounded and mixed with Muslim neighborhoods, the "mountains" are Palestinian territory: instead of saving themselves they would be going to certain death. The Palestinians are not "the Gentiles" but the Philistines (flishtim, sons of Casluhim, of Ham's descent); You can't even talk about "those from Judeah", because Jews no longer live in Judeah, that territory is under international control according to the UN treaty, and is called the West Bank, with non-Jewish occupation. The situation of Jerusalem in the days of Vespasian are different from the context in which it will be when the Antichrist manifests itself.

Even Revelation 11:2 points out that "the Gentiles" will trample on Jerusalem for 42 months, saying nothing of "abomination", nor "desolation", nor defeat, nor flood (metaphorical or literal), nor destruction of a third temple or of its desecration (so much so that it says that the interior "is not touched"), nor of the expulsion of the Jews (as Yeshua does say, that they would be taken to the nations, as actually happened), nor of fleeing, nor of destroying completely, only to "tread" (drill) the city. That is to say, there will be war, and Jerusalem will have it within its borders, but all the rest of the issues referred to in the other prophecies do not coincide or correspond to this conflict, only the pattern of 3 and a half years that is always repeated and the fact of an Israeli conflict. In this sense, neither did Daniel or Yeshua say anything in these prophecies that two prophets would come, nor did Daniel say anything corresponding to everything that John did affirm about the Apocalypse. That text from the eschatological sermon is talking about the abomination of devastation over Judeah almost 2,000 years ago, not something future, and it is believed to be future because it is read mixed with the theme of the great tribulation. Why are they both together? Because it was a conversation where Jesus answered two different things that his disciples asked him: the prophetic topic about Jerusalem and Judeah, and apart, the signs of his coming.

Simple examples, making comparative prophecy, we know that other prophets announced the war of the Kidron and Har-Magedon:

northeast and center of Israel, which will be the important points of the conflict, beginning with the war in Jerusalem, focused on the Kidron valley, and later the magnified war in the valley of Megiddo. On the other hand, Zacarías does not say anything about abomination or desolation. Because? Because as John says in Revelation, the "interior" (the area of the holy place) is not touched or desecrated. Jerusalem will have war especially in Kidron, and the city will have war, yes, but the holy place will not be touched, as it was touched in the past. That is, there will be no abomination. She will have difficulties but in the end she will be victorious, that is, no situation will leave her desolate (deserted) or devastated, as it did in the 2nd century AD. C. Abomination is the desecration of holy things or the practice of unworthy things; Desolation or Desolation is to destroy something and leave it deserted. There were many abominations and few desolations, but only one event that had both. Israel will be attacked, especially Jerusalem, but not necessarily all of Judeah, as happened in the Abomination of Desolation, because Judeah today is the West Bank, non-Jewish territory. Jerusalem will be attacked, but there will be no abomination, nor will the conflict reach the point of leaving it desolate, because the Lord will save his people this time.

Among the notable differences between the abomination of 168 B.C. C. and that of the year 66-70 d. C. is that the Romans were not interested in the issues of the temple, but in the revolt, while Antiochus IV did want what was inside the temple, and used bribes, agreements and the same force to get away with it . In the first of the two cases, after 2,300 "ereb boker" (afternoon-morning) the temple was purified and consecrated, celebrating that important day to this day as the Hanukkah festival, one of the most important celebrations in Judaism; In the second case, things did not end well: the temple and the city were destroyed, and in the end everyone was expelled from Judeah. Comparing this with the predictions about Revelation, nothing is said about the desecration of the temple or the destruction of the Jews or that by their own strength they will be able to definitively get rid of their enemies (they will have courage in their god, but it will be their God who will give them victory , literally speaking). By the time of Jesus, the desecration of Antiochus had already occurred, that is, by saying, " *of which Daniel spoke* ", he was referring, in effect, to one whose context was to come, and which occurred 30 years after those words. (began at that time and ended in the year 135 AD).

" *But when you see the abomination of desolation that Daniel the prophet spoke of, placed where it should not be (he who reads, understand), then those who are in Judea flee to the mountains.* " (Mark 13:14-18)

By emphasizing, " *put where it should be (he who reads understands)* ", he wants to emphasize, because many Jews thought - and even today they want to think - that the end of Daniel 9 alludes to the idolatrous imposition perpetrated by Antiochus in 168 a. . C., since "abomination" (Shikutz, in Hebrew) refers to idolatry in a holy place (the temple), but as we know Jerusalem has not had a temple since 70 AD. C. The word "meshomem" and "mishmem" (desolate or devastating) does not fit in the context of the year 168 a. C., but yes from the year 66 d. C. As well announced by Yeshua (Jesus), those who were specifically in Judeah had to flee to the mountains, because the site that the legions of Vespasian caused was in Jerusalem, capital of Judeah at that time. And the legions V Macedonica, XII Fulminata, XV Apollinaris and X Fretensis surrounded the city and took the Mount of Olives, after the northern regions had been subdued after the revolts of the Zealots.

When Yeshua said that the flight should be at that moment, it was a strategic matter, because before it was not necessary or prudent, since the troops came from different points, and it was to take Jerusalem that they came by the known route from the north and then surrounded it . That, as Yeshua says and Josephus agrees, was on Easter, since the people had gone up to Jerusalem for the feast. Since the siege was intended to control the Jewish revolt after Nero's death, it was safe for people to stay on the roof of their houses, but if they were in the city it was best to flee, and of course, if they were working in the fields it was better . It was logical not to return to their homes or to the city. Obviously this context has nothing to do with the future war of the nations against Israel, because it will be all the nations against Israel, not several Roman legions, and they will take over the cities, the streets, the mountains and the fields as an invasion. It won't do any good to go to the mountains, because, furthermore, today, those mountains no longer exist, nor do the groves that in the past would have been a refuge for someone. In fact Israel is prepared for this, among other things, with miklat (bunkers) in each house and building, so if a woman is raising or pregnant, she should only go down to hide in the miklat (where she has supply of services (bathrooms).), ventilation, water, food and electricity). Not the same, in the past this would be horrendous escaping on foot or by donkey, and worse, outside the two or three common routes that would be controlled (that is, fleeing steep slopes and mountains and without water sources in the middle of the desert). .

Another point is that the siege lasted for more than 3 years, and people couldn't get out of the wall because they were surrounded, and there was no way to get the excrement out, nor for food or water to enter. This Roman strategy was intended to weaken them and lead them to surrender. At the point that winter when they found a weak point in the wall that they burst - and entered - came the worst of the massacre (a million Jews and proselytes were massacred in the streets, in the houses and in the temple, which was set on fire). If one looks at Joel's prophecies about the Third World War, or those of Zacharias, Isaiah and Ezekiel, among others, about the Fourth World War, none of them say anything about "winter", "Easter", "flee to the mountains", etc But if you read the Maccabees and Josephus, you see that those episodes did fit into contexts from that time. The Great Tribulation - which is before the war in har-Magedon and Cedron - will affect Israel little or nothing, and the later one does not give the option of fleeing out of the city.

If there was going to be an invasion 30 years after Yeshua left, and they could be in danger, it is logical that he would warn them, which he did, but he also told them about the Antichrist and his return. There were things mixed up in the dialogue of the Eschatological Sermon, firstly because those who listened and/or wrote it, did not even know yet the prophecy of the Apocalypse, nor the gross context of the "finmundista" theme. During what I call "World War III and World War IV", the Jews will not be able to flee anywhere, and it is important to understand all this to put aside old and incorrect biblical interpretations that confuse and distance our understanding from seeing reality. what is actually going to happen.

A) The Israelis will be surrounded by all the surrounding towns, beginning with the neighborhoods of Palestinian communities with which we cohabit. There is nothing outside of Israel that is safer than Israel itself, even less if "leaving" means going to hostile territories, which are those that surround Israel. B) The desert is not the safest place to hide, let alone the mountains. The safest thing to do is to hide in the miklat (bunkers) and let the IDF (Israel Defense Forces) handle the war. C) The rooftops will not be safe (before they were, when there were no rifles, grenades, missiles and other surveillance systems and explosives), nor the open field, but the refuge areas that my country (Israel) has, and has been implementing since the 50s. D) There are no "Judean mountains"... they are small hills that today belong to Palestinian, West Bank and Jordanian territory (enemies of Israel). E) The Romans, Babylonians, Syrians and Egyptians captivated and enslaved people, but in the war against Israel there will be no hostages, because the radical Islamists do not have this perspective, they are going to kill, and they are not organized as nations with their rights policies for hostages. For this reason, in previous works , such as

'Remote Vision', I explain the other part of this dialogue of Yeshua in its true apocalyptic section.
Blessings.

[]

Don't miss out!

Visit the website below and you can sign up to receive emails whenever Frederick Guttmann publishes a new book. There's no charge and no obligation.

https://books2read.com/r/B-A-DKUGB-QLKAF

BOOKS 2 READ

Connecting independent readers to independent writers.

About the Author

Israeli writer, researcher, disseminator, documentary filmmaker and influencer. He is the writer of more than 35 books, mostly research and dissemination theses.

Read more at https://www.frederickguttmann.com.